MADE IN CZECHOSLOVAKIA
Book 2

By Ruth A. Forsythe

Photography by David E. Richardson

Items on front and back covers are illustrated and described under the appropriate categories.

Published by

ANTIQUE PUBLICATIONS
P.O. Box 553
Marietta, Ohio 45750

©Copyright 1993 by Antique Publications

PB ISBN# 0-915410-98-2

Dedicated
To All Who Love
Beautiful Things

NOTES

CONTENTS

ACKNOWLEDGEMENTS

The author sincerely thanks her family and friends for their support and encouragement while writing this book.

A special thank you to the wonderful people who shared their knowledge of the subject; the many who contributed excellent examples to be photographed, and the very astute proofreaders. Their time, trust and unselfishness will never be forgotten. They are as follows:

Marilyn Anderson - The Best of Both Worlds - Ohio

Jim Cooper - Ohio

Robin and Neil Denker - California

Mindy Forsythe - Ohio

Ellen Foster - California

Ron and Cheri Heimbach - Pennsylvania

Stephen Kraynak - Ohio

Lisa Lippsett - New York

Sylvia Massenelli - Ohio

Mr. and Mrs. Bill Mrazek - Virginia

Ronn Perrin - Ohio

Viola Potts - Ohio

Betty Rains - Ohio

Teri Sell - Ohio

Lois Sipher - Ohio

Mr. and Mrs. Andrew P. Show, Jr. - Ohio

Lucille Show - Ohio

Donna G. Sims - Ohio

Kathleen Steele - Ohio

Mr. and Mrs. Daniel Van Horn - Ohio

Patricia Wunderle - Ohio

INTRODUCTION

My first book, *Made in Czechoslovakia*, published in 1982, illustrates 674 pieces of glass with an addenda of 74 pieces of pottery and porcelain.

This book, *Made in Czechoslovakia,* Book 2, illustrates 672 pieces of pottery and porcelain, with an addenda of 343 glass perfume bottles.

The significance of the books is to give recognition to the artistic products exported to the United States from Czechoslovakia from 1918 to 1938.

The Czechs and Slovaks settled in Bohemia centuries ago. They were discontent with the Austrian and Hungarian form of government and were desirous of a country of their own.

When World War I began, the Czechs and Slovaks in France, Russia and the United States, organized military units to fight with the Allies. The war ended in 1918 and the Czechs and Slovaks dream came true. Bohemia, Moravia and Austrian Silesia were given to the Czechs and Slovaks and at last they had a country of their own, named Czechoslovakia.

The new country of Czechoslovakia was smaller than the state of New York, but boasted hundreds of glass and china factories. China tableware was made in great quantities and shipped to America. After 1918 it was no longer labeled Austria, Bohemia or Carlsbad china, it was labeled Czechoslovakia.

Immediately, Czechoslovakia came to be known as a well-developed cultural center. Their arts had been carefully fostered from the very beginning of their history. Despite its small size, the Czech nation was of the first rank in industrial art. Prague, the capital of Czechoslovakia, and now the capital of the Czech. Republic, is still considered one of the most important cultural centers in the world.

There have been many changes in Czechoslovakia since 1938. During 1938, to pacify Hitler, the western end of Czechoslovakia was given to Germany and other territory to Hungary and Poland. In 1939, Hitler invaded Czechoslovakia, but at the end of World War II, Czechoslovakia's original boundaries were returned. In 1948, Czechoslovakia became Communist controlled and was called Republic of Czechoslovakia. December of 1989 marked the end of communism in Czechoslovakia. January 1, 1993 Czechoslovakia split into two independent states, Czech Republic and Slovak Republic.

I sincerely hope that my books will assist collectors in recognizing the many unique and artistic objects made in Czechoslovakia. There will be no more.

HOW TO USE THIS BOOK

All headings are listed on contents page.

Measurements are height except, plates are diameter and platters and hand mirror are length.

All measurements are approximate.

Every item is numbered. References are made to item number, page number or mark number and each reference will be designated item, page or mark.

A picture is worth a thousand words, therefore, descriptions of all items are brief.

Following are hand drawn marks to be found on Czechoslovakian Pottery, Porcelain and Perfume Bottles. All marks are surface ink stamped unless noted otherwise ( ).

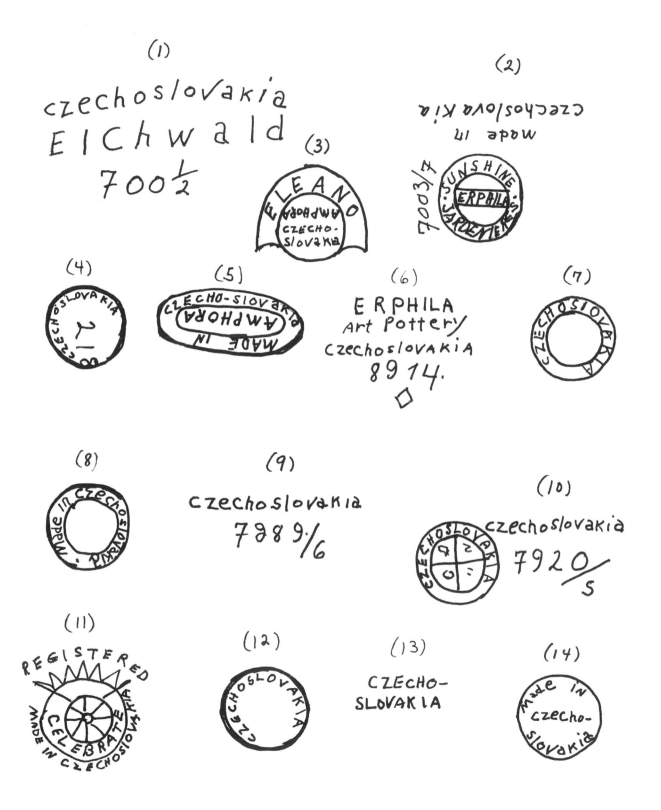

(1) czechoslovakia EIChwald 700½

(2) Made in czechoslovakia 7003/7 SUNSHINE JARDENIER ERPHILA

(3) ELEANO AMPHORA CZECHO-slovakia

(4) CZECHOSLOVAKIA 2 700

(5) CZECHO-slovakia MADE IN AMPHORA

(6) ERPHILA Art Pottery czechoslovakia 8914.

(7) CZECHOSLOVAKIA

(8) Made in czechoslovakia

(9) czechoslovakia 7889/6

(10) CZECHOSLOVAKIA czechoslovakia 7920/5

(11) REGISTERED CELEBRATE MADE IN CZECHOSLOVAKIA

(12) CZECHOSLOVAKIA

(13) CZECHO-SLOVAKIA

(14) Made in czecho-slovakia

(15)

MADE IN
CZECHOSLOVAKIA

(16)

CHELSEA

(17)

MZ
Altrohlau
CM-R
CZECHOSLOVAKIA
Eden

(18)

OMECO
made in
Czecho.Slovakia

(19)

TK
Thun
Bohemia
Czechoslovakia
BORDEAUX

(20)

TK
Thun
Czechoslovakia
EDNA

(21)

V
made in
Czechoslovakia

(22)

PHOENIX CHINA
CZECHO-SLOVAKIA

(23)

VICTORIA
CZECHO-SLOVAKIA

(24)

ERPHILA
ART POTTERY
Czechoslovakia
383

(25)

Czechoslovakia
Hand-painted

(26)

CZECHOSLOVAKIA

(27)

CZECHO
SLOVAKIA

(28)

CZECHO
F
B S
SLOVAKIA

(29)

Hand. Painted
DITMAR-URBACH
Z
MADE IN CZECHOSLOVAKIA

(30)

ERPHILA
CZECHOSLOVAKIA

(31)

Epiag
CZECHOSLOVAKIA
V

(32)

made in Czechoslovakia
276

(33)

MADE IN CZECHOSLOVAKIA

(34)

VICTORIA
Czechoslovakia

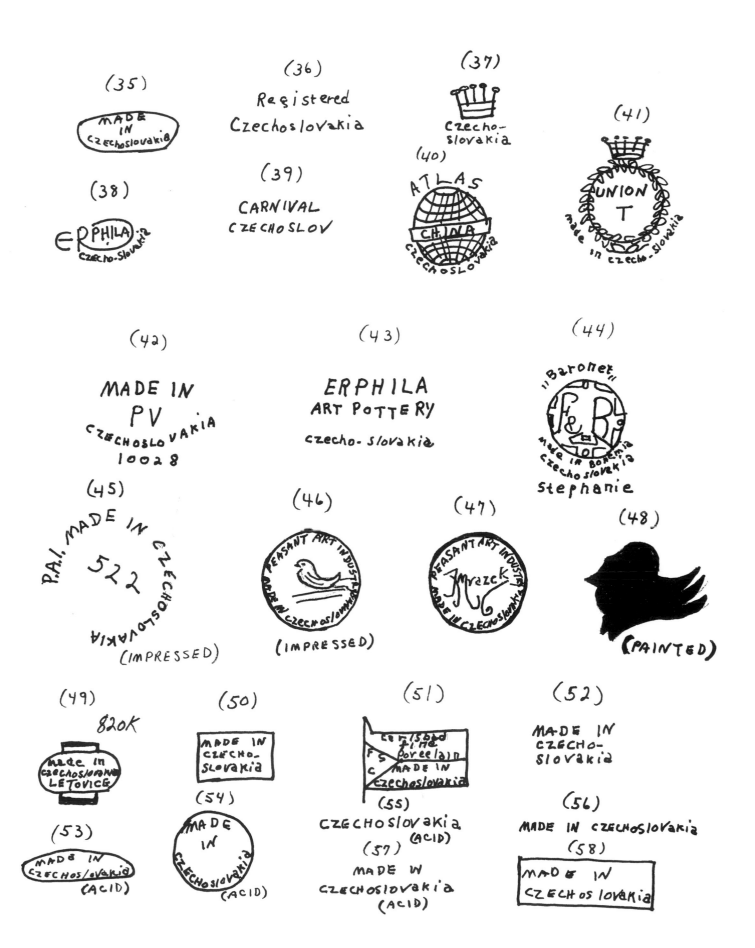

(35) MADE IN CZECHOSLOVAKIA

(36) Registered Czechoslovakia

(37) Czecho-Slovakia

(41) UNION T made in czecho-slovakia

(38) ERPHILA CZECHO-SLOVAKIA

(39) CARNIVAL CZECHOSLOV

(40) ATLAS CHINA CZECHOSLOVAKIA

(42) MADE IN PV CZECHOSLOVAKIA 10028

(43) ERPHILA ART POTTERY czecho-slovakia

(44) "Baronet" FeB made in Bohemia czechoslovakia Stephanie

(45) P.A.I. MADE IN CZECHOSLOVAKIA 522 (IMPRESSED)

(46) PEASANT ART INDUSTRY MADE IN CZECHOSLOVAKIA (IMPRESSED)

(47) PEASANT ART INDUSTRY Mrazek MADE IN CZECHOSLOVAKIA

(48) (PAINTED)

(49) 820K made in CZECHOSLOVAKIA LETOVICE

(50) MADE IN CZECHO-Slovakia

(51) Carlsbad fine Porcelain FSC MADE IN Czechoslovakia (ACID)

(52) MADE IN CZECHO-Slovakia

(53) MADE IN CZECHOSlovakia (ACID)

(54) MADE IN CZECHOSlovakia (ACID)

(55) CZECHOSlovakia (ACID)

(56) MADE IN CZECHOSlovakia

(57) MADE IN CZECHOSLOVAKIA (ACID)

(58) MADE IN CZECHOSlovakia

11

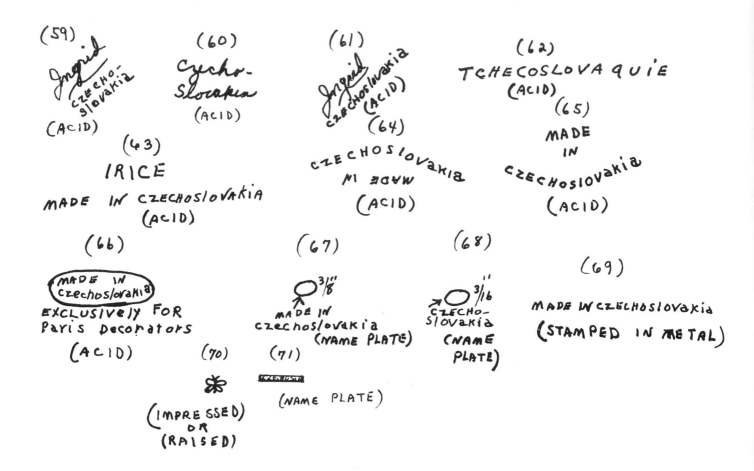

(59) *Ingrid* CZECHO-slovakia
(ACID)

(60) Czecho-Slovakia
(ACID)

(61) *Ingrid* CZECHoSlovakia
(ACID)

(62) TCHECOSLOVAQUIE
(ACID)

(63) IRICE
MADE IN CZECHOSLOVAKIA
(ACID)

(64) CZECHOSLOVAKIA
MADE IN
(ACID)

(65) MADE IN CZECHOSLOVAKIA
(ACID)

(66) MADE IN Czechoslovakia
EXCLUSIVELY FOR Paris Decorators
(ACID)

(67) 3/8" MADE IN Czechoslovakia
(NAME PLATE)

(68) 3/16" CZECHO-Slovakia
(NAME PLATE)

(69) MADE IN CZECHOSlovakia
(STAMPED IN METAL)

(70)
(IMPRESSED) OR (RAISED)

(71)
(NAME PLATE)

PEASANT ART – An expression of what is beautiful, appealing; more than ordinary.

We think of Peasant Art as country art and of the colorful embroidery designs on clothing worn by the Czechoslovakian peasant. However, this form of art was far reaching and was used to decorate the home exterior and interior, furniture, lamps, dishes and furnishings in general.

Prominent among the artists who led in evolving design ideas for the peasant artisans was Joseph Mrazek, who originated the buoyant colorful pottery which became recognized everywhere as typical of the vital spirit of the Czech race. The older pottery had been somewhat lacking in brilliant tones and Mrazek envisioned the charm of harmonized florid tones, used in juxtaposition, as the distinctive flower or fruit motifs which are so well known.

Joseph Mrazek was born in 1889 in Podebrady, Czechoslovakia, about fifteen miles southwest of Prague. He was apprenticed to an artist when very young. When in his teens, he came to the United States to live on an uncle's farm in South Dakota. In his late teens, he attended the St. Louis Academy of Art and made his way to New York City intent on a career in the arts. He went to work for the Hester Decorating Company, which sent him and other artists, to Boston to create murals for Child's restaurants. After a period in Boston, Mrazek returned to New York to pursue his work in the arts.

He married Ada Miksickova in 1912.

Joseph's pottery industry had its beginning in 1917 when he saw a Macy's advertisement for ceramic paints. One could paint an object and they would fire it in a kiln on the store premises. Mrazek soon mastered the technique and bought his own kiln and set it up in the kitchen of his Yorkville apartment on the upper east side. He became intrigued with the prospect of art pottery as a business venture and began searching the bins and vendors' wheelbarrows on Delancy Street for inexpensive crockery to bring home for decorating. He even purchased some pottery marked "Made in Japan". He painted a bird over the mark on the underside of the pottery when he decorated the piece. In this book (1) (2) and (3) are marked on the underside in this manner.

Joseph Mrazek found there was a great demand for his product. So great, that he decided to rent a factory in his homeland in Letovice, Province of Moravia, Czechoslovakia. There were nearby clay mines, inexpensive fuel and a pool of ceramic workers. Business was so good that in 1925 he built his own factory and in 1926, enlarged the factory.

Mrazek designed the Letovice factory, machinery for preparing clays and glazes was bought. He trained his workers to execute his designs in the folk art tradition. He designed his own molds to form the basic clay bodies that were later hand finished on a potter's wheel. The wares of the Peasant Art Industries were exported to the United States for quality retail outlets and department stores such as Marshall Fields.

His wife Ada's business and administrative abilities made it possible for her to run the factory in Czechoslovakia. She and son Bill stayed in Czechoslovakia while Joseph concentrated on design and sales in the United States. He traveled to Czechoslovakia about three times a year to supervise operation of the factory. The name of the company was Czecho Peasant Art Co., Inc., 10 West 19th Street, New York City.

Peasant Art Industries' pottery was awarded a gold medal at the 1926 Fair in Philadelphia.

In keeping with the times, art deco was a popular subject along with the bird and the fruit and flower patterns. Numerous items were made such as lamps, plates, bowls, vases, pitchers, mugs, cups and saucers, clocks and other items. Parchment type lamp shades were made to match some of the lamps. Brilliant colors were used such as yellow, orange, scarlet, blue, green and purple.

Joseph Mrazek loading his kiln in his Yorkville apartment. This was the beginning of a successful business in making and marketing Peasant Art Pottery.

The factory closed in 1933 due to the world wide depression.

After World War II, Joseph and Ada lived in Centerport, Long Island. He died in 1959, she in 1973.

Peasant Art Industries was not alone in the making of peasant art in Czechoslovakia. There were a number of factories in Czechoslovakia exporting peasant art to the United States and other countries. Consequently, many fine pieces are to be found that were made by others. The problem in the future is going to be to find the very decorative peasant art.

PEASANT ART, PROVINCIAL AND ART DECO – An Exquisite Combination

Peasant Art Lamps, a Provincial wine jug, an Art Deco bowl and more. All this and as usual, wild with color.

AMPHORA AND AMPHORA TYPE – Beautiful and Mysterious

Amphora made before 1918, is marked Austria. After that time, Czechoslovakia.

Amphora was originally a two-handled, narrow-necked vessel which was large in the center and narrow at the base. It was used by the ancient Greeks and Romans for holding wine, oil, and other liquids. The Austrian and Czechoslovakian Amphora was designed to be artistic and beautiful as well as useful.

Amphora can be found in high glaze or mat finish and often a combination of both. Interesting shapes in vases, pitchers, planters, baskets and figurals were made. As with most Czech, Art Deco style is evident. Not to be left out is the Egyptian influence because of the opening of Tutankhamen's Tomb in 1922-23. Birds, animals, people and flowers are other subjects used to enhance Amphora.

MAJOLICA – Elaborate Designs and a Brilliant Luster

Majolica has a heavy glaze and is decorated with bright colors. It is said to have originated in the 1500's on the Spanish island of Majorca.

Majolica was very popular during the Victorian era and was made by most countries of the world.

There was another revival in the 1920's and the Czechs exported quantities to the United States. There were many large and elaborate objects made in Czechoslovakia. So large, that they came in sections and were bolted together. Small pieces, ash trays, bowls, pitchers, ink wells, wall pockets and others, were made in abundance.

LAMPS – A Combination of Style and Beauty

Lamps were made in most categories – Peasant Art, Amphora and Amphora Type, Art Pottery, People, Animals, Birds, and Children. Sometimes, the finial was just as interesting as the lamp.

ART DECO AND NOVELTY – Color and Plenty of It

This section is crammed full of unusual examples of Czech ingenuity. A goat pitcher, a bird pitcher, a duck planter, pitchers, tumblers, water sets with fruit, snack sets, tea sets, wall pockets, stacked tea pots, a pitcher with a bird perched on the handle, an ash tray and cigarette box with a girl's head in relief and much more. All of this in exciting colors like yellow, orange, scarlet, blue, green and colorful florals.

ART POTTERY AND OTHER – Browns, Blacks, Tans and many Tasteful Combinations

Many pieces were done in the silhouette manner. An abundance of Erphila was made.

PEOPLE, ANIMALS AND BIRDS, AND MORE – Interesting Figurals

This section is full of birds, cows, people and very desirable cream and sugar sets.
There are 15 different bird wall pockets, chickens, a deco cat, a zebra, covered ducks, salt and pepper sets, creamers, large and small figural birds, clocks, book ends and several figurines.

LUSTER AND IRIDESCENT AND OTHER – Beautiful

The beautiful luster and iridescent in just about everything. A bridge set with plates shaped like heart, diamond, club and spade. Clocks, canisters, vases, sugar and creamers, tea sets, plates and more.
Luster and iridescent were very popular during the 1920's and early 1930's.

MISCELLANEOUS

Vases, book ends, cups, baskets and candle holders.

CHILDREN AND OTHER

Baby plates, tea sets and lamps

DINNER SETS – Beautiful and Useful

The dinner sets came in service for 4, 6, 8 or 12 and open stock. These were very popular as home entertaining was in vogue at that time. Most dinner sets were of fine porcelain, but there were some made in semi-porcelain. Many of the sets included the name of a girl as part of the makers' mark on the underside of the pieces. I have seen Sylvia, Edna, Stephanie, and Edith. Some patterns were names such as Iris, Eden, Royal Bohemia and Royette. However, most sets only have the factory name and Made in Czechoslovakia on the back. The semi-porcelain set in this book is called Chelsea.

KITCHEN
Canister or kitchen sets as they were called, came in a complete set of 15 pieces. There were juicers, sea food dinner sets, fruit plates and more.

PERFUME BOTTLES – Elegant

Anything written about Czechoslovakian exports to the United States from 1918 to 1938, would not be complete without the exceedingly popular perfume bottles. Superior quality, style and beauty made them a fashionable item of the period. They are now fervently sought after by collectors and for the same reasons.

There are many different styles in clear crystal, colored crystal and opaque colors. Unique bottles and stoppers, combinations of bottles and stoppers and colors continue to surface. The addition of brass, enamel and jewel ornamentation, causes a bottle to look entirely different.

Since the old advertisements of Czechoslovakian perfume bottles name only a few colors, the collectors and writers are determining the color of many bottles. Colors are in the many shades of red, amber, green, blue, pink, clear crystal and various opaque colors. As more styles are found, so are more colors, such as opaque tan, opaque brown and opaque pink.

As a result of the bottles having been around for so many years, many are found with minor damage such as small chips, broken applicators or stoppers that do not fit properly. One reason for the stopper not fitting properly, may be that the bottle is from a set. The stoppers were ground individually to fit the bottle. Sometimes, in use, stoppers from sets were switched. One should not turn down a bottle for reasons that do not affect its beauty.

An example of a bottle and stopper not being original mates is item (932). However, there were so many different combinations that one cannot be positive about any of them being wrong. If the bottle is Czechoslovakian, the stopper is Czechoslovakian, the color combination is correct, there is balance and conformity, and both are of the same time period, chances are they belong together. If the bottle looks right, it probably is right.

Beware of reproduction Czechoslovakian stoppers. They are easy to spot because of poor quality. Sometimes stoppers are used that are not Czechoslovakian and they, too, are easily detected.

Most of the brass and jewel ornamentation was made in Czechoslovakia. The only exceptions are Austria or France. In this book, they are noted in the descriptions.

Marks are in the marks section of this book and they are (53) through (71). The majority of the bottles are marked with one of the following. An acid stamp on bottom of the bottle, or occasionally on the smooth surface of the stopper or side of the bottle. A tiny intaglio or raised butterfly on either the bottle or the stopper. The brass and jewel ornamentation is marked with a small brass name plate or Czechoslovakia stamped in the metal. Some of the ornamentation is not marked in any way.

While information regarding individual factories is scarce to non-existent, we do know of the Hoffman factory (Mark 70) and the Ingrid bottles made by Hoffman's son-in-law, marks (59) and (61). The Hoffman and Ingrid bottles are indicated in the descriptions. Their quality is superb.

The bottles with figural nude applicators are very scarce as are many of the figurals and opaques.

There are hundreds or even thousands of different Czechoslovakian perfume bottles that were produced during the 1918 through 1938 time period. This makes them a wonderful collectable since there is a choice of size, color or subject. Examples of the contrasts in variety are items (999) through (1015). A collector may choose to collect plain or fancy, figural, floral, geometric, mythological, animal, insect, cut glass, plain but polished all over, and in every color imaginable and sizes ranging from mini to large. Many bottles are scarce. However, none are common.

For a more in depth study of Czechoslovakian perfume bottles, I suggest the book: *Czechoslovakian Perfume Bottles and Boudoir Accessories* by Jacquelyne Y. Jones-North, Antique Publications, Box 553, Marietta, OH 45750.

DUŠAN JURKOVIČ.   94.

BEMALTES HAUS
IN PETROVÁ VES.

MALOVÁNÍM ZDOBENÁ
CHALUPA V PETROVÉ VSI.

FERME PEINTE À
PETROVÁ VES.

Photos, Courtesy of Bill Mrazek

Above, are three views of a simple dwelling either in the country or part of a small village. The home was usually of one story, and subdivided into three rooms, the living room, kitchen and storeroom. The simplicity of architecture is balanced by the decorative effect of painted designs. These are used to beautify the walls inside and out, especially about the doors and windows.

The native pieces of furniture of the humble dwelling – beds, chests, chairs, cupboards, tables and wardrobes – were made of soft wood and generally brightly colored and painted with peasant designs. Circa 1925.

Decorators working in the Letovice factory PEASANT ART POTTERY

Above, son Bill lends a helping hand. PEASANT ART POTTERY

JOSEPH MRAZEK
DESIGNER OF
CZECHO-PEASANT
CERAMIC ART
AT WORK
IN HIS STUDIO
AND SOME
OF HIS DESIGNS

Above are many examples of the artistic creations of Joseph Mrazek

Registered July 27, 1926.   **Trade-Mark 215,882**

UNITED STATES PATENT OFFICE.

CZECHO PEASANT ART CO. INC., OF NEW YORK, N. Y.

ACT OF FEBRUARY 20, 1905.

Application filed April 2, 1926. Serial No. 229,547.

STATEMENT.

To all whom it may concern:

Be it known that Czecho Peasant Art Co. Inc., a corporation duly organized under the laws of the State of New York, located in the borough of Manhattan, city, county, and State of New York, and doing business at 8 West 19th Street, in said city, has adopted for its use the trade-mark shown in the accompanying drawing.

The trade mark has been continuously used in its business and of its predecessor in foreign and interstate commerce since December, 1922.

The particular description of goods to which the trade mark is appropriated is POTTERY, comprised in Class 30, Crockery, earthenware, and porcelain.

The trade mark either displayed alone or in association with other matter, is displayed by printing the same on labels which are placed within the goods or affixed to packages containing the goods, or by displaying the same on the goods themselves. The trade mark is not limited to any particular color or combination of colors.

CZECHO PEASANT ART CO. INC.,

By MILADA JARUSEK,

Secretary and Treasurer.

Photo, Courtesy of Bill Mrazek

All the Peasant Art in this book was not the work of Joseph Mrazek. Many factories in Czechoslovakia and other countries made Peasant Art Pottery. So many copied the Mrazek patterns that Joseph was forced to take out patents to protect his designs. Above is an example of one of the patents.

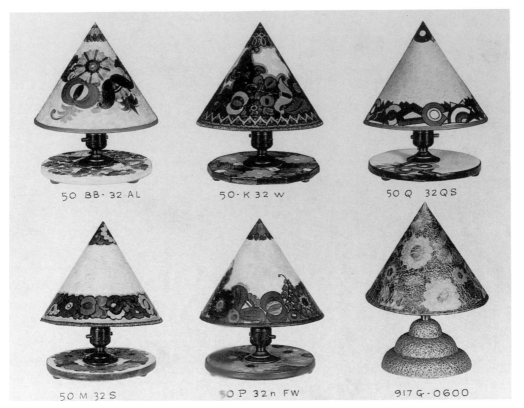

50 BB-32 AL   50-K 32 W   50 Q 32QS

50 M 32 S   50 P 32n FW   917 G-0600

Photo, Courtesy of Bill Mrazek

710 DB 202 F W   643T 25 JCR   679 K 25 FW

647 Q 36Q   635 C 25 W   900 B-0620

Photo, Courtesy of Bill Mrazek

Czechoslovakian Peasant Art Lamps worth looking for. Almost impossible to find with the original shades.

Advertising for Czecho Peasant Art Co., Showing the best known mark used by the company.

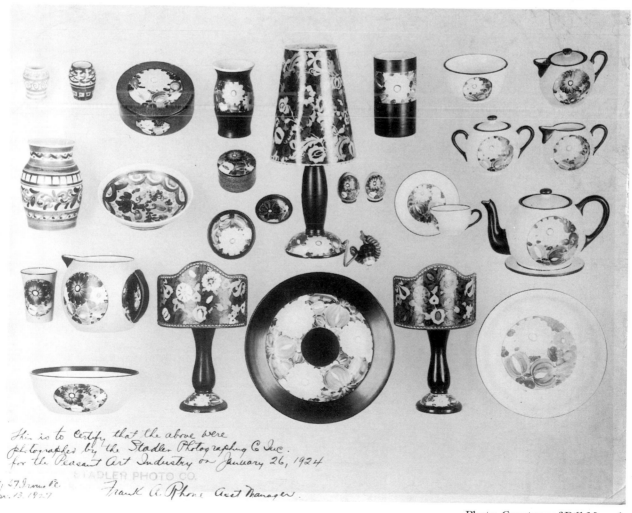

Beautiful pieces sold by Czecho Peasant Art Co.

The color photographs to follow will show that Czechoslovakians loved brilliant colors, but at the same time they catered to the quiet and subdued and even snow white.

Most designs were noticeably artistic and imaginative. However, a few were more commonplace.

The cities reflect the best of the professional arts of modern Europe -- architecture, painting, sculpture, literature and opera, so one is rather surprised to discover that the folk arts are the richest and most interesting of their kind in all Europe.

Letovice factory built and painted by Joseph Mrazek

More beautiful pieces of Mrazek Peasant Art. Note the Peasant Art lamp and shade.

An elaborate ad by the Czecho Peasant Art Co., Inc. Mrazek circle trade mark was not the only one used. There were earlier marks showing a painted bird and another showing an impressed bird. These marks are shown in the section on Czechoslovakian marks.

26

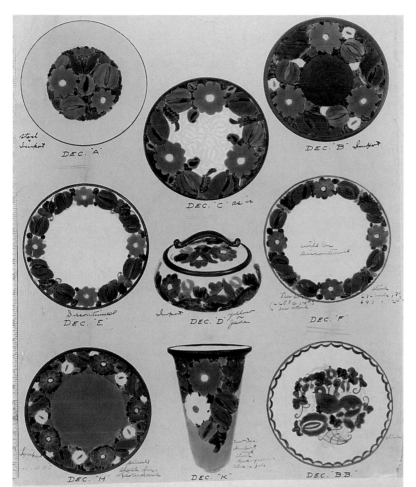

PEASANT ART POTTERY

Examples of Peasant Art more difficult to find

Photo, Courtesy of Bill Mrazek

Photo, Courtesy of Bill Mrazek

(1) 6" Pitcher, Black & Yellow Border
(2) 4¼" Mug – Matches Pitcher (1)
(3) 14" Round Tray – Matches (1) and (2)
(4) 7" Covered Pitcher, Yellow, Flower and Fruit Motif
(5) 7" Covered Pitcher, Scarlet, Flower and Fruit Motif
(6) 7" Covered Pitcher, Black, Flower and Fruit Motif

(7) 7" Plate, Blue, Flower and Fruit Motif
(8) 7" Covered Pitcher, Blue, Flower and Fruit Motif
(9) 5" Creamer, Yellow, Flower and Fruit Motif
(10) 4½" Creamer, Green, Flower and Fruit Motif
(11) 5½" Milk Pitcher, Blue Bird Motif
(12) 5" Covered Pitcher, Blue with Orange Trim — Floral

(13) 8" Plate, Scarlet, Flower and Fruit Motif

(14) 7½" Vase, Green, Flower and Fruit Motif

(15) 6½" Pitcher, Blue, Flower and Fruit Motif

(16) 12" Plate, Green, Flower and Fruit Motif

(17) 7½" Vase, Scarlet, Flower and Fruit Motif

(18) 4" Bowl With Lid, Yellow, Flower and Fruit Motif

(19) 4½" Sugar Bowl, Orange, Flower and Fruit Motif

(20) 3½" Creamer, Orange, Flower and Fruit Motif

(21) 8¼" Chocolate Pot, Orange, Flower and Fruit Motif

(22) 4¼" Bowl, Yellow, Flower and Fruit Motif

(23) 8" Plate, Scarlet, Flower and Fruit Motif

(24) 3¼" Creamer, Scarlet, Flower and Fruit Motif

(25) 3½" Sugar, Scarlet, Flower and Fruit Motif

(26) 3" Creamer, Blue, Flower and Fruit Motif, Painted Underglaze, Rare!

(27) 3½" Sugar, Blue, Flower and Fruit Motif, Painted Underglaze, Rare!

(28) 5" Covered Bowl, Cream, Flower and Fruit Motif, Painted Underglaze, Rare!

(29) 4" Mayonnaise, Green, Flower and Fruit Motif

(30) 10½" Clock, Blue, Flower and Fruit Motif
(31) 5" Creamer, Scarlet, Flower and Fruit Motif
(32) 11½" Plate, Scarlet, Flower and Fruit Motif
(33) 8½" Vase, Scarlet, Flower and Fruit Motif
(34) 2½" Ash Tray, Blue, Flower and Fruit Motif
(35) 6½" Tea Pot, Blue, Flower and Fruit Motif
(36) 3½" Egg Cup, Blue, Flower and Fruit Motif
(37) 5" Sugar, Blue, Flower and Fruit Motif
(38) 4¼" Creamer, Blue, Flower and Fruit Motif

(39) 2½" Box, Blue, Flower and Fruit Motif
(40) 3½" Sugar, Blue, Flower and Fruit Motif
(41) 2½" Salt and Pepper, Blue, Flower and Fruit Motif
(42) 4" Box, Blue, Flower and Fruit Motif
(43) 3" Candle Holder, Blue, Flower and Fruit Motif
(44) 2¼" Cup and Saucer, Blue, Flower and Fruit Motif

(45) 7½" Plate, Scarlet, Flower and Fruit Motif

(46) 2½" Cup and Saucer, Black, Flower and Fruit Motif

(47) 2½" Cup and Saucer, Green, Flower and Fruit Motif

(48) 9½" Plate, Scarlet, Flower and Fruit Motif

(49) 2½" Ash Tray, Orange, Flower and Fruit Motif

(50) 4" Bell, Black, Flower and Fruit Motif

(51) 2" Pair of Candle Holders, Yellow, Flower and Fruit Motif

(52) 4½" Mug, Scarlet, Flower and Fruit Motif

(53) 4½" Covered Bowl, Scarlet, Flower and Fruit Motif

(54) 1½" Bowl, Yellow, Flower and Fruit Motif

(55) 3" Box, Scarlet, Flower and Fruit Motif

(56) 2½" Box, Yellow, Flower and Fruit Motif

(57) 3" Match Holder, Green, Flower and Fruit Motif

(58) 3½" Coaster, Black, Flower and Fruit Motif

(59) 1¼" Bowl, Green, Flower and Fruit Motif

(60) 4" Creamer, Blue, Flower and Fruit Motif

(61) 3" Box, Scarlet, Flower and Fruit Motif

(62) 7½" Lamp, Black, Flower and Fruit Motif
(63) 12" Plate, Blue, Flower and Fruit Motif
(64) 10" Lamp, Yellow, Art Deco Motif Peasant Art
(65) 7" Hot Plate, Multi-Color
(66) 7½" Vase, Black, Flower and Fruit Motif
(67) 4½" Vase, Cream, Blue Bird Motif
(68) 4½" Vase, Black, Flower and Fruit Motif

(69) 8½" Jug, Provincial, White Floral
(70) 8¼" Plate, Blue, Flower and Fruit Motif
(71) 3½" Bowl, Purple and Yellow Art Deco
(72) 3½" Candle Holders, Green, Flower and Fruit Motif
(73) Covered Bowl, Green, Flower and Fruit Motif
(74) Footed Bowl, Black, Flower and Fruit Motif

75

(75) 20½" Vase, Pastel Colors, Amphora, Cherubs,
   Flowers and Blue Ribbon

(76) 12" Basket, Rust, Amphora
(77) 9½" Planter, Pink, Jewels, Amphora
(78) 10¼" Vase, Tan, Amphora
(79) 11¼" Vase, Tan, Stork, Amphora
(80) 6¼" Jardinier, Tan, Amphora
(81) 8½" Pillow Vase, Blue, Amphora Type
(82) 8" Jardinier, Yellow, Sculptured Birds,
    Amphora

(83) 7" Bowl Vase, Rose, Amphora Type, Eleanor
(84) 6½" Vase, Gray, Amphora
(85) 3" Bowl, Gray, Jewels, Amphora
(86) 7¼" Vase, Tan, Amphora
(87) 7" Vase, White, Amphora

(88) 10½" Covered Jar, Yellow, Sculptured Fox, Amphora

(89) 14" Pitcher Vase, Pink, Amphora

(90) 9½" World Lamp, Yellow, Amphora, New Shade

(91) 7½" Basket, Blue, Amphora

(92) 6½" Basket, Blue with Butterfly, Amphora

(93) 5½" Basket, Blue, Amphora

(94) 6" Sugar Bowl, Green, Amphora

(95) 3½" Planter, Yellow, Sculptured Goat, Amphora

(96) 3½" Open Sugar, Multi-colored, Amphora

(97) 3½" Pair Sculptured Fish Candle Holders, Amphora

(98) 9½" Vase, Cream, Egyptian, Amphora Type
(99) 9" Vase, Cream, King Tut, Amphora Type
(100) 10" Lamp, Cream Egyptian, Amphora Type, New Shade
(101) 8½" Double Candle Holder, Amphora Type Erphila Art Pottery, Isabel
(102) 7½" Vase, Tan, Isabel and Colom, Amphora Type

(103) 7½" Pitcher Vase, Tan, Amphora Type
(104) 6" Pitcher, Tan, Amphora Type
(105) 6½" Candy, Tan, Amphora Type, Erphila Art Pottery
(106) 4½" Jardinier, White, Amphora Type, Erphila Art Pottery

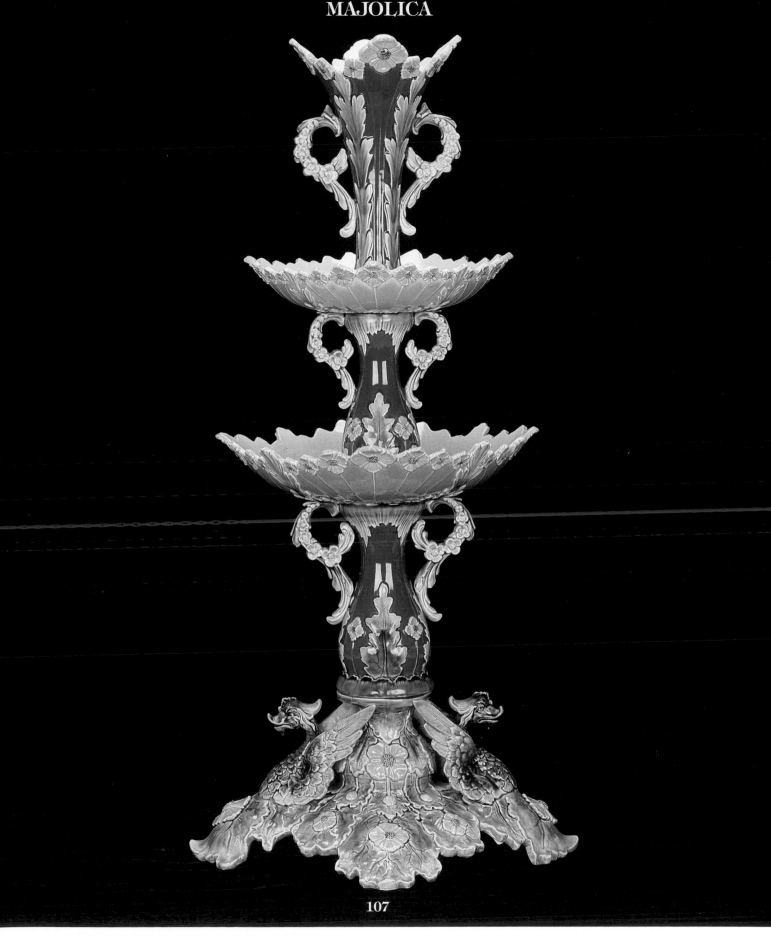

107

(107) 34" Epergne, Purple, Pink, Yellow and
    Green. Six pieces bolted together.

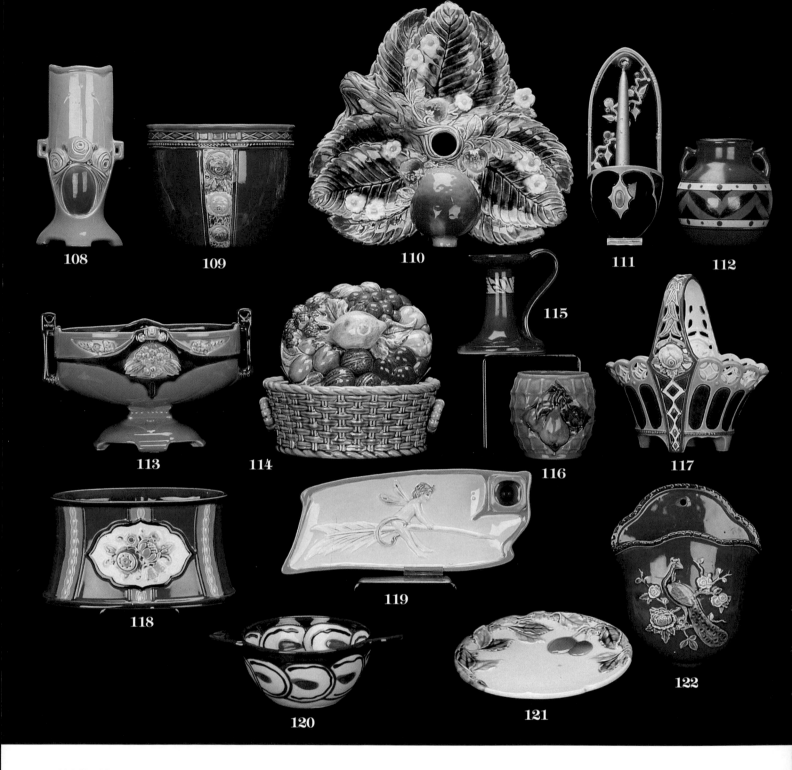

(108) 8" Vase, Yellow, Majolica

(109) 5½" Jardinier, Blue, Majolica

(110) 11½" Strawberry Dish with Strawberry Sugar Shaker, Majolica

(111) 9" Wall Candle Holder, Black, Majolica

(112) 5" Vase, Scarlet, Hand Painted

(113) 5" Handled, Footed, Oblong Bowl, Purple, Majolica

(114) 4¼" Handled Basketweave Bowl with Fruit Lid, Majolica

(115) 4" Candle Holder, Purple, Hand Painted

(116) 4" Vase, Blue, Majolica

(117) 7½" Basket, Purple, Majolica

(118) 4½" Letter Box, Blue, Majolica

(119) 2¼" Ink Well Tray, Yellow, Majolica

(120) 2½" Bowl, Yellow, Majolica

(121) 7" Plate, Cream, Majolica

(122) 7½" Wall Pocket, Blue, Majolica

LAMPS

123

124

(123) 12½" Lamp, Black, Peacock Motif with Jeweled Peacock Finial, New Shade

(124) 12½" Lamp, Dark Blue Luster with Matching Ball Finial, New Shade

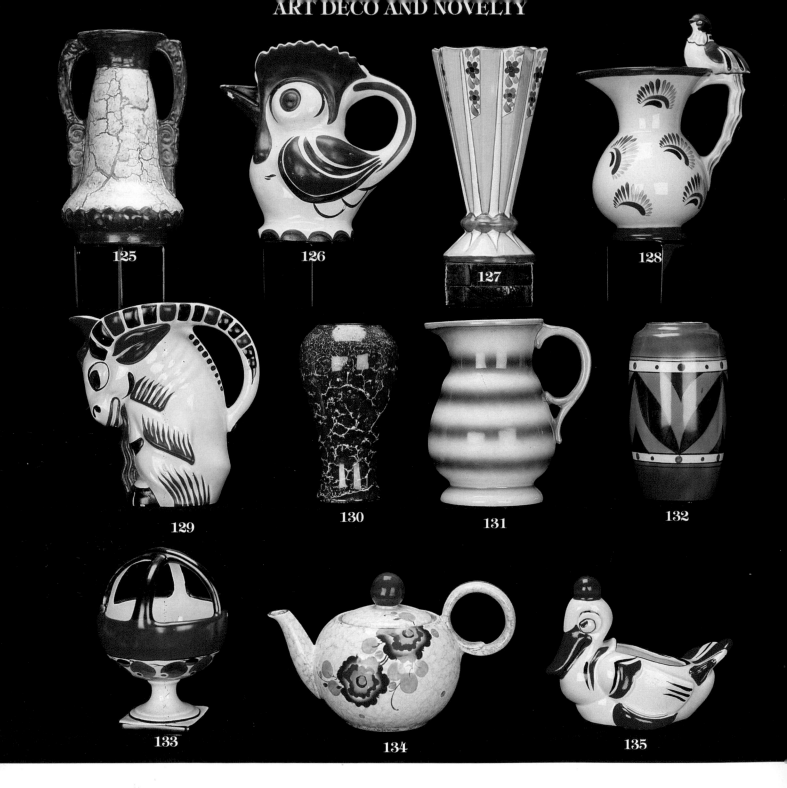

(125) 10" Handled Vase, Cream and Scarlet
(126) 9¼" Bird Pitcher, Yellow and Red
(127) 9½" Vase, Yellow and Floral
(128) 10½" Pitcher, Yellow, Bird Perched on Handle
(129) 8½" Pitcher, Goat, Yellow and Red
(130) 8" Vase, Red

(131) 8" Pitcher, Purple Stripes
(132) 7½" Vase, Scarlet and Green
(133) 7¼" Handled Basket, Scarlet and Yellow
(134) 5½" Tea Pot, Marbled White with Scarlet Finial, Very Art Deco
(135) 5½" Duck Planter, Yellow and Scarlet

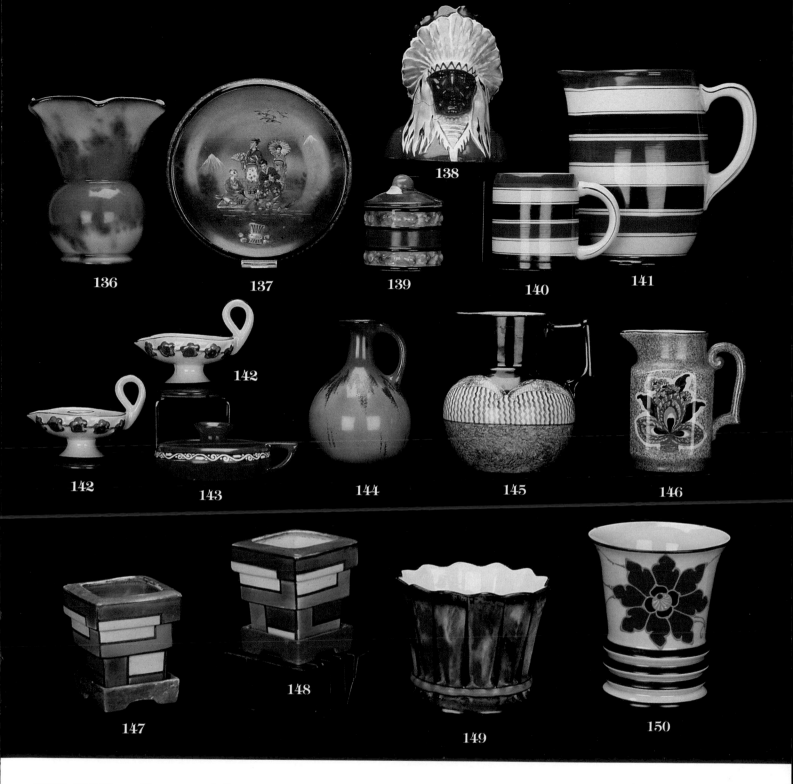

(136) 7½" Vase, Orange and Gray
(137) 2" Bowl, Oriental Motif
(138) 7½" Book End, Indian, Scarlet and Gray
(139) 4" Mustard, Scarlet
(140) 4½" Mug, Scarlet, Black and White
(141) 9" Pitcher, Scarlet, Black and White
(142) 4" Candle Holders, Pr. Yellow
(143) 2" Candle Holder, Scarlet

(144) 6½" Pitcher, Orange and Blue
(145) 7" Pitcher, Black and Blue
(146) 6¼" Pitcher, Orange
(147) 4½" Flower Pot, Blue
(148) 4½" Flower Pot, Orange
(149) 7" Planter, Multi-Color
(150) 6¾" Flower Pot, Yellow

(151) 8" Pitcher, Orange Handle
(152) 11½" Plate, Blue Rim
(153) 6¾" Pitcher, Orange Handle
(154) 7¼" Cookie Jar, Scarlet
(155) 3½" Tumbler, Orange and Blue
(156) 8¼" Wall Pocket, Orange Flower
(157) 7" Wall Pocket, Orange Flower

(158) 4½" Creamer, Scarlet, Cherries
(159) 7" Watering Can, Orange
(160) 6½" Tea Pot, Orange Flower
(161) 4¼" Creamer, Orange Flower
(162) 2" Cup and Saucer, Orange Flower
(163) 4½" Basket, Scarlet
(164) 4¾" Sugar, Orange Flower

165

166

167

168   169   170   171   172

173   174   174   175   176   177

(165) 9½" Plate, Niagara Falls, Iridescent Yellow and Blue
(166) 3" Large Bowl, Floral, Pierced Border
(167) 10½" Plate, Orchid Motif
(168) 6" Vase, Burgundy Flower
(169) 9" Pitcher, White with Festive Motif
(170) 5½" Urn Vase
(171) 7" Vase

(172) 6" Vase, Rose Decoration
(173) 2¼" Porcelain Box
(174) 3½" Powder Box, Shown Open to Reveal Painting Inside Box
(175) 2½" Porcelain Box, Blue
(176) 3¾" Mug with Festive Motif
(177) 3¾" Mug with Festive Motif

178 179 180 180 181 180 180

182 183 184 185 186

187 188 189 190 191

(178) 8" x 12½" Tray, Grapes and Flowers
(179) 9½" Pitcher with Lid, Grapes and Flowers
(180) 4" Tumblers, Scarlet and Yellow
(181) 8½" Pitcher, Scarlet and Yellow
(182) 7½" Pitcher, Yellow and Green
(183) 5½" Pitcher, Blue
(184) 8¼" Handled Vase, Black and Multi-Colored

(185) 8" Pitcher, Yellow and Blue
(186) 7" Vase, Cream
(187) 7¼" Wall Pocket, Orange
(188) 8" Wall Pocket, Scarlet
(189) 3¼" Box, Cream and Orange
(190) 5" Mustard, White, Pear Finial
(191) 6¼" Pitcher, Scarlet

(192) 8½" Snack Plates and Cups, Orange and Blue Flowers

(193) 7¼" Vase, Scarlet

(194) 2½" Bowl, Yellow

(195) 5¼" Basket, Green

(196) 4" Oblong Bowl, Green

(197) 2" Bowl, Green

(198) 6¾" Cookie Jar, Magenta

(199) 2¾" Cup and Saucer, Scarlet, Yellow and Black

(200) 5¾" Stacked Teapot, Cream and Sugar; Matches (192)

(201) 6¼" Pitcher, Black and Orange

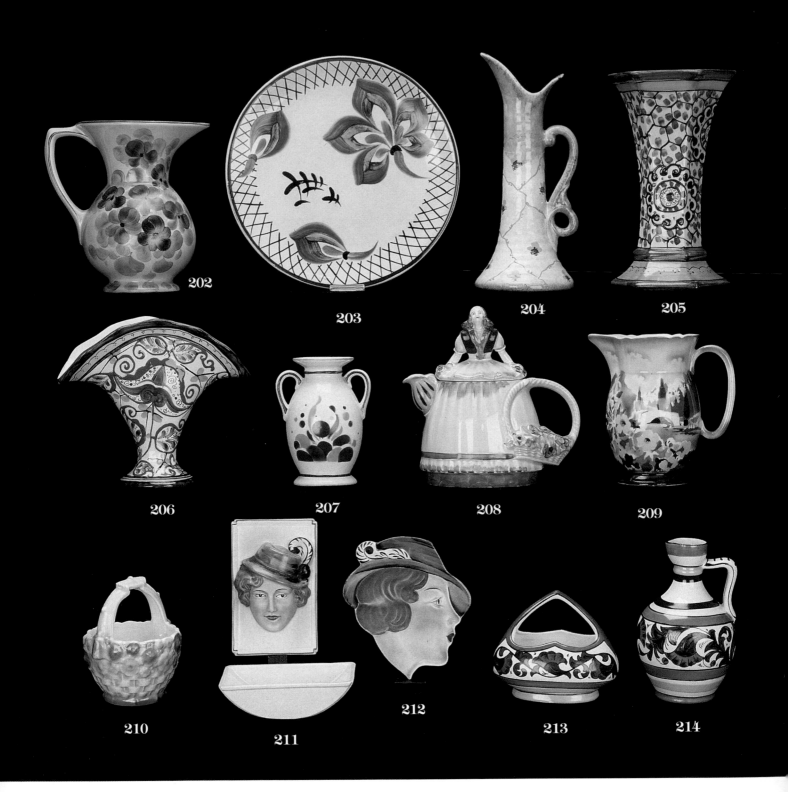

(202) 7¾" Pitcher, Green Blue and Orange Floral

(203) 10½" Plate, Orange and Yellow Flower and Leaf

(204) 11" Ewer, Gold and Lavender Color

(205) 10" Vase, Orange and Blue

(206) 7½" Fan Vase, Blue, White and Orange Paisley Type Design

(207) 5¾" Handled Vase, White with Art Deco Motif

(208) 8¼" Teapot, Cream, Sculptured Figure Lid

(209) 6½" Pitcher, Scenic and Floral

(210) 5¼" Basket, Yellow with Band of Flowers

(211) 3" Cigarette Box, Cream, Sculptured Figure Lid

(212) 1" Ash Tray, Cream, Companion to (211)

(213) 5" Basket, Yellow and Orange, Paisley Type Design

(214) 6½" Pitcher Jug, Yellow and Orange, Paisley Type Design

ART POTTERY AND OTHER

(215) 10¼" Vase, House and Garden, Art Pottery
(216) 10½" Handled Vase, Multi-Color
(217) 5½" Covered Creamer, Erphila, Art Pottery
(218) 5¼" Wall Pocket, Erphila, Art Pottery
(219) 3¾" Candle Holder, Erphila, Art Pottery
(220) 4" Creamer, Erphila, Art Pottery
(221) 5" Jardiniere, Silhouette, Erphila, Art Pottery

(222) 8" Vase, Silhouette, Erphila, Art Pottery
(223) 12½" Lamp, Scenic, Art Pottery, New Shade
(224) 8" Vase, Scenic, Art Pottery
(225) 5½" Vase, Multi-Color Erphila, Art Pottery
(226) 7½" Cookie Jar, Erphila, Art Pottery, Silhouette
(227) 4¼" Creamer, Purple
(228) 4" Mug, Scarlet, Silhouette

(229) 6½" Candle Holders, Pair, Butterfly
(230) 5½" Vase, Brown, Portrait
(231) 8¼" Pitcher, Blue, Couple
(232) 6¾" Pitcher, Brown, Couple with Sheep
(233) 7¼" Pitcher, Green, Boy with Sheep
(234) 6" Vase, Brown, Portrait
(235) 8" Vase, Green and Gold Color, House, Horse and Wagon
(236) 8½" Vase, Brown, Two Women

(237) 8", Handled Vase, Green, Rose and Rosebud
(238) 7½" Pitcher, Brown and Yellow, Little Bo-Peep
(239) 8" Handled Vase Green, Silhouette
(240) 4½" Creamer, Green, Floral
(241) 4" Sugar Bowl, Brown, Floral
(242) 4¼" Fan Vase, Blue
(243) 4¼" Vase, Brown, Floral
(244) 5" Bell, Lady
(245) 4½" Covered Jar

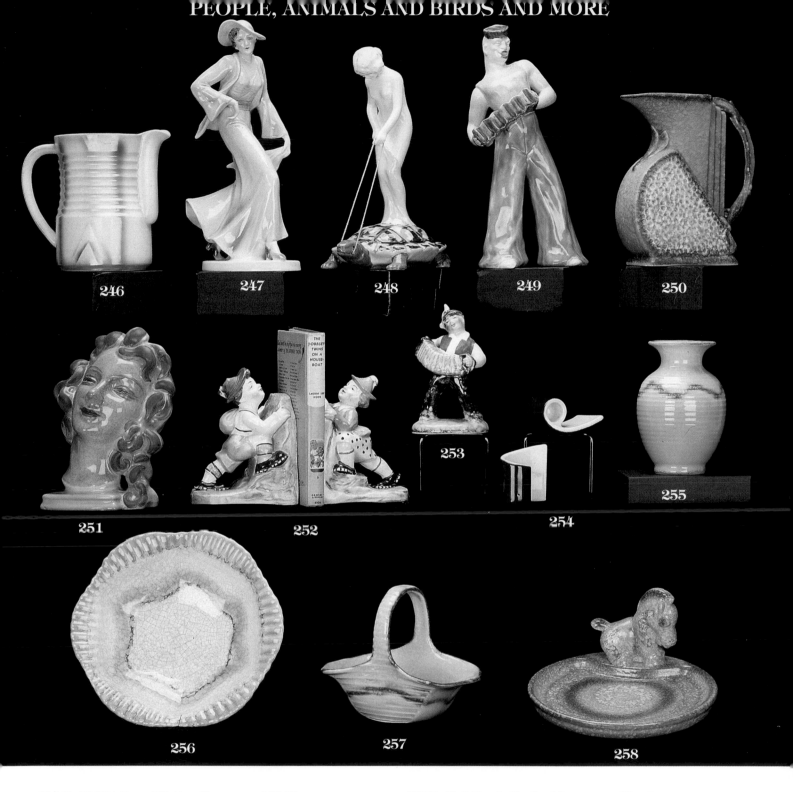

(246) 6" Pitcher, White, Green and Yellow
(247) 11½" Figurine of 1920's Lady
(248) 10½" Figurine, Girl Riding a Turtle Flower Frog
(249) 11½" Figurine, Sailor
(250) 8" Pitcher, Aqua and Tan
(251) 8" Girl with Red Hair

(252) 6¼" Book Ends, Mountain Climbers
(253) 5½" Figurine of Man
(254) 2½" Pr. of Candle Holders, Maroon
(255) 6" Vase, Blue and Yellow
(256) 2½" Bowl, Blue and White
(257) 5½" Basket, Blue and Yellow
(258) 4½" Card Tray, Blue and Yellow

49

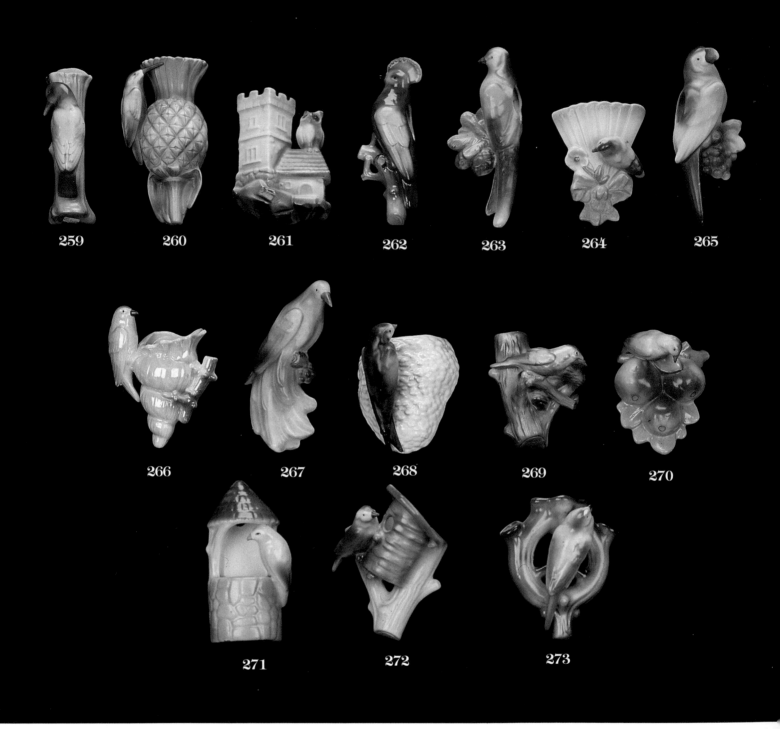

(259) 6¾" Wall Pocket, Woodpecker
(260) 7" Wall Pocket, Bird and Pineapple
(261) 5½" Wall Pocket, Owl
(262) 7½" Wall Pocket, Bird
(263) 8" Wall Pocket, Bird
(264) 5" Wall Pocket, Bird with Fan
(265) 7¾" Wall Pocket, Parrot
(266) 6" Wall Pocket, Bird and Sea Shell, Luster Finish

(267) 7" Wall Pocket, Bird and Berry
(268) 5" Wall Pocket, Bird on Honeycomb
(269) 4¾" Wall Pocket, Bird and Nest
(270) 5¼" Wall Pocket, Bird and Apples
(271) 6¼" Wall Pocket, Bird at Wishing Well
(272) 6" Wall Pocket, Bird at Nest
(273) 5½" Wall Pocket, Bird and Branch

(274) 6¾" Hen, Orange and White

(275) 7" Rooster, Orange and White

(276) 6¼" Chicken, Orange and White, Erphila

(277) 6¼" Chicken, Orange and White, Erphila

(278) 9" Rooster, Blue, Orange and White

(279) 3" Piggy Bank, Tan

(280) 5½" Cat, Cream, Green Eyes

(281) 5" Duck, Covered Serving Dish, Blue

(282) 3" Chick, Individual Serving Dish, Yellow

(283) 6½" Zebra, Brown, Gray and Green

(284) 3½" Dog Ash Tray, Yellow and Gray

(285) 3" Duck, Individual Serving Dish, Blue. A Companion to (281)

(286) 6" Cow Pitcher, Orange

(287) 4¾" Cow Creamer, Brown

(288) 6" Cow Pitcher, Brown

(289) 4½" Cow Creamer, Brown Spots

(290) 4½" Cow Creamer, White, Orange Spots

(291) 4¼" Cow Creamer, Orange

(292) 4¼" Cow Creamer, Orange, Blue and Yellow Spots

(293) 5½" Swan Pitcher, Blue and White

(294) 7½" Canister, Blue and White, Oatmeal

(295) 6" Hand Painted Tile

(296) 4¼" Swan Planter, White

(297) 6" Hand Painted Tile

(298) 6" Pitcher, Blue and White, George Washington, Erphila

(299) 4¾" Creamer, Bird, Yellow, Green and Orange

(300) 5¼" Pitcher, Swan, Gold and White

(301) 4½" Creamer, Parrot, Brown

(302) 4¼" Jardiniere, Cherries, Erphila Art Pottery

(303) 4½" Basket, Niagara Falls, Green and Yellow with Bird

(304) 4½" Creamer, Parrot, Orange

(305) 4" Individual Teapot, Tan

(306) 3½" Creamer, Moose Head, Brown

(307) 4½" Basket, Green and Yellow with Bird

(308) 4" Napkin Ring, Girl, Erphila

(309) 4¼" Duck Planter, White Erphila

(310) 2" Salt and Pepper, Horses, Tan

(311) 3" Salt and Pepper, Flower Pots, Lavender and White

(312) 4¼" Box, Duck, Brown and Cream

(313) 3" Chick, Individual Serving Dish, Yellow

(314) 3¼" Salt and Pepper, Bashful Boy and Girl, Blue and Orange

(315) 3" Salt and Pepper, Mexican, Scarlet, Yellow and White

(316) 4" Creamer, Scarlet, Erphila

(317) 3½" Creamer, Scarlet, Erphila

(318) 3" Creamer, Scarlet, Erphila

(319) 4" Pitcher, Blue and White

(320) 3¼" Creamer, Blue and White

(321) 3¾" Creamer, Tan and Brown

(322) 4" Duck, Covered Sugar, Green, Brown and Yellow

(323) 4" Duck Creamer, Green, Brown and Yellow; Matches (322)

(324) 4¼" Potato, Individual Baked Potato Server, Light Brown

(325) 4¼" Covered Sugar, Strawberry with Strawberry Finial, Scarlet

(326) 3¾" Creamer, Strawberry, Scarlet, Companion to (325)

(327) 2½" Open Sugar, Carnival

(328) 4½" Creamer, Carnival, Companion to (327)

(329) 3" Covered Tomato, Scarlet

(330) 4" Covered Apple, Scarlet

(331) 3¼" Swan Covered Sugar, White

(332) 3¼" Swan Creamer, White, Companion to (331)

(333) 2½" Open Sugar, Grape, Blue, White and Green

(334) 4" Creamer, Grape, Blue, White and Green, Companion to (333) Grape Leaf Spout

(335) 2" Open Sugar, Grape, White

(336) 4¼" Creamer, Grape Leaf Spout, White, Companion to (335)

(337) 3½" Creamer, Scarlet, Polka Dot

(338) 8" Salt Box, Nude Child on Tree Limb, Eichwald
(339) 7" Salt Box, Bird Motif
(340) 3¼" Moose Creamer, Brown and Blue
(341) 5¼" Moose Creamer, Brown and Blue
(342) 3¾" Moose Creamer, Brown
(343) 4" Moose Creamer, Brown and Blue
(344) 4¾" Creamer, Mexican, White, Scarlet and Yellow
(345) 4¾" Creamer, Nun, Scarlet and White
(346) 6" Pitcher, Woman, Orange and White
(347) 5" Creamer, Mrs. Gamp, Scarlet and White
(348) 4" Creamer, Blue and Yellow

(349) 2" Creamer, Scarlet, Black and Yellow
(350) 2" Creamer, Green
(351) 6" Pitcher, Blue, Yellow and White
(352) 3¼" Creamer, Sam Weller, Blue, Erphila
(353) 4" Creamer, Scarlet and Black, Buckingham Palace Guard
(354) 3½" Ash Tray, Yellow and White
(355) 4" Ash Tray with Match Holder, Yellow, Blue and Black
(356) 8" Toothbrush Holder, Lady, White, Erphila
(357) 4¼" Pipe Holder, Yellow and Tan
(358) 3½" Ash Tray, Jester, Blue and White

54

359

360

361

362

363

364

365

366

367

368

369

370

371

372

373

(359) 9" Parrot, Green, Scarlet and Blue, Figurine
(360) 8" Vase, Yellow and Green
(361) 12" Double Vase, Vulture, Green and Black
(362) 9¾" Vase, Heron, Black and White
(363) 10" Parrot, Scarlet, Blue and Black, Figurine
(364) 5¼" Flower Holder, Green on White Ball
(365) 5¼" Flower Holder, Brown and Yellow
(366) 5½" Flower Holder, Scarlet and Green

(367) 5½" Flower Holder, Scarlet and Green
(368) 5" Flower Holder, Tan
(369) 5¼" Flower Holder, Scarlet, Blue and Green
(370) 5" Flower Holder, Scarlet and Green
(371) 5¼" Flower Holder, Scarlet and Brown
(372) 8¾" Parrot, Blue, Green and White, Figurine
(373) 5¼" Flower Holder, Blue and Brown

(374) 12¾" Lamp Base, Vulture, Green and Gray

(375) 11½" Clock with Birds, Cream and Brown

(376) 9" Figurine, Parrot, Green and Blue

(377) 12½" Heron, Black and Green

(378) 6¼" Flower Holder, Green and Brown

(379) 5" Flower Holder, Bird, Green

(380) 5¾" Flower Holder, Bird, Brown and Yellow

(381) 5½" Flower Holder, Bird, Blue and Green

(382) 5¾" Flower Holder, Bird, Green and Yellow

(383) 5½" Flower Holder, Bird, Blue, Yellow and Green

(384) 5½" Flower Holder, Bird, Yellow and Green

(385) 4¾" Flower Holder, Bird, Blue and Gold

(386) 4¼" Flower Holder, Bird, Brown and Yellow

(387) 4" Flower Holder, Bird, Green and Pink

(388) 3¾" Flower Holder, Bird, Rose, Yellow and Gray

(389) 3½" Flower Holder, Bird, Blue and Brown

(390) 4" Flower Holder, Bird, Green and Rose

(391) 2¾" Figurine, White

(392) 2¾" Figurine, White

(393) 4¾" Figurine, Pheasant, Orange, Blue, Yellow and Gray

(394) 6¼" Book Ends, Horse Head, White
(395) 7" Figurine, Bull Dog, Brown and White
(396) 10" Figurine, Lady, White
(397) 8¼" Figurine, Madonna and Child, White
(398) 8¼" Vase, Figure, White
(399) 5¼" Single Book End, Child, Yellow and White
(400) 5¼" Handled Vase, White with Lavender
Flowers
(401) 5" Figurine, Child with Umbrella, Scarlet,
Blue and Yellow
(402) 6" Figurine, Child, White
(403) 6" Figurine, Child, White

(404) 5½" Basket, Taupe and White
(405) 4¼" Figurine, Monkey, White
(406) 4" Figurine, Horse, Blue
(407) 3¾" Figurine, Horse, White
(408) 4¼" Cigarette Box, Horse Finial, White
(409) 3¾" Flower Holder, Elephant, Yellow and
White
(410) 3½" Ash Tray, Sail Boat, Blue, Green and
Orange
(411) 2½" Ash Tray, Horse, White
(412) 4¾" Watering Can, White with Lavender
Flowers

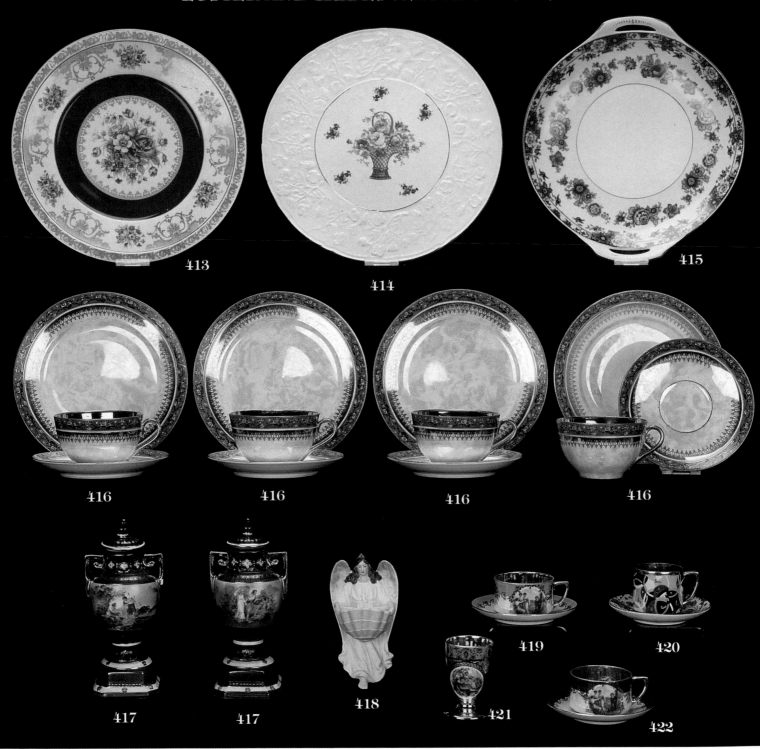

(413) 10½" Plate, Floral with Maroon Band

(414) 10¾" Plate, White with Multi-Colored Basket of Flowers

(415) 11" Plate, Open End with Floral Motif

(416) 7½" Plates, 2" Cups and Saucers, Set of Four, Iridescent Body with Band of Blue

(417) 7" Pair of Urns, Portrait and Scenic with Blue and Gold

(418) 5¾" Font, Bisque, Angel, Blue and White

(419) 2" Cup and Saucer, Mini, Portrait, Green and Iridescent

(420) 2½" Cup and Saucer, Mini, Black, Orange, Yellow and Gray

(421) 3" Egg Cup, Portrait, Green and Gold with Gold Interior

(422) 2" Cup and Saucer, Mini, Portrait, Blue and Iridescent

(423) 3" Salt and Pepper, Pink Luster with Cameos
(424) 5" Vase, Lavender and Green Luster
(425) 4¾" Syrup, Lavender Luster with White Iridescence
(426) 4¼" Sugar, Rose Luster
(427) 3" Creamer, Rose Luster
(428) 5½" Teapot, Rose Luster
(429) 5" Covered Sugar, Orange Luster, White Iridescence
(430) 4" Creamer, Orange Luster, White Iridescence
(431) 6¼" Pair Candlesticks, Tan Luster

(432) 4¼" Basket, Tan Luster
(433) 5" Basket, Orange Luster with Blue Rim
(434) 3" Cow Creamer, White Luster with Orange Handle
(435) 4" Teapot, White Iridescence, Black Trim
(436) 3" Moose Creamer, White Luster, Scarlet Handle
(437) 4¼" Basket, White Luster, Orange Trim
(438) 4¼" Covered Sugar, White Iridescence, Black Trim
(439) 4¼" Creamer, White Iridescence, Black Trim

59

(440) 4¾" Sugar, Iridescent Yellow Inside, Iridescent White on Exterior, Gold Trim

(441) 2½" Cups and Saucers (4) Iridescent Yellow Inside Cups Iridescent White Exterior of Cups and Saucers, Gold Trim

(442) 3" Creamer, Iridescent Border, Yellow Chicks

(443) 3¾" Creamer, Iridescent Yellow Inside, Iridescent White on Exterior, Gold Trim

(444) 5½" Teapot, Iridescent Yellow Inside, Iridescent White on Exterior, Gold Trim

(445) 6½" Stacked Teapot, Sugar and Creamer, Butterscotch, Luster

(446) 2½" Bowl, Exotic Bird, Tan and White, Luster

(447) 4¼" Sugar, Covered Butterscotch, Luster

(448) 3¼" Creamer, Butterscotch, Luster

(449) 7½" Plates, Iridescent White, Gold Trim. Goes with (440) (441) (443) (444) A Set

(450) 4¾" Basket Flower Frog, Blue and Gold, Luster

(451) 3¾" Creamer, Butterscotch Luster, Blue and Red Bands

(452) 3" Salt, Pepper and Mustard on Tray, Butterscotch, Luster

(453) 7¾" Plate, Exotic Bird, Butterscotch and White, Luster

(454) 3¾" Creamer, Tan with Green Handle, Luster

(455) 2½" Cup and Saucer, Butterscotch Luster

(456) 7½" Plate, Butterscotch Luster

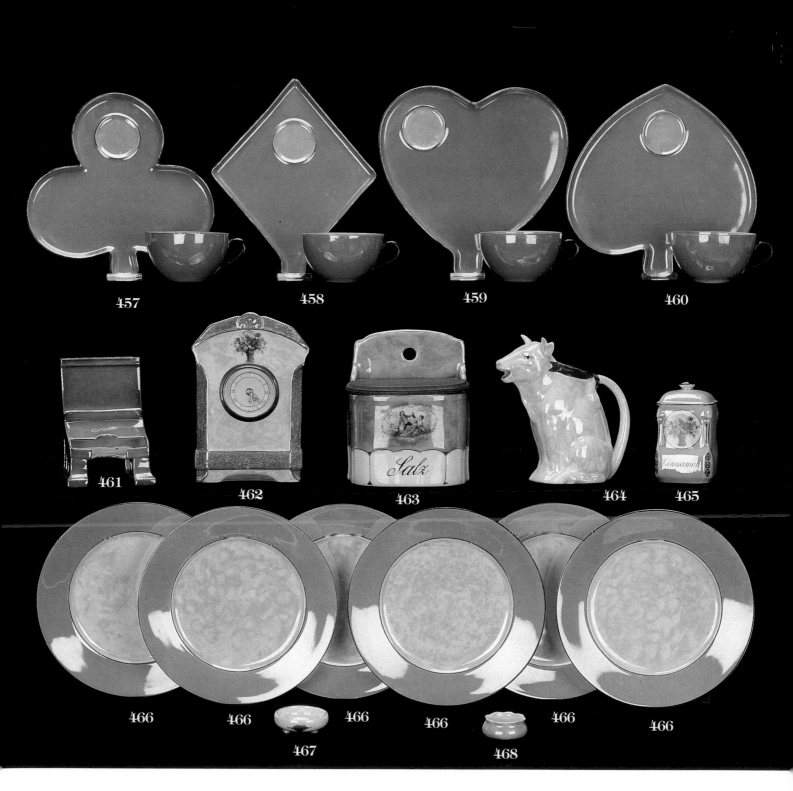

(457) 9" Club Plate with Cup, Blue and Tan Luster
(458) 8¼" Diamond Plate with Cup, Blue and Tan Luster
(459) 8½" Heart Plate with Cup, Blue and Tan Luster
(460) 8½" Spade Plate with Cup, Blue and Tan Luster
(461) 5¼" Match Holder, Blue Luster
(462) 7" Clock, Blue Luster and White Iridescent, Basket of Flowers
(463) 6¼" Salt Box, Blue Iridescent with White, Portrait of a Man and Woman

(464) 6¼" Cow Pitcher, White Iridescent with Blue Trim
(465) 4½" Cinnamon Jar, Blue Luster with Basket of Flowers
(466) 8" Plates (6) Blue Luster Rim with White Iridescent Centers
(467) 2" Salt Dip, White Iridescent
(468) 1½" Salt Dip, Blue Luster with Inside of Green Luster

(469) 7½" Canister, White Iridescent, Barley, Floral Motif

(470) 7½" Canister, White Iridescent, Tea, Floral Motif

(471) 7½" Canister, White Iridescent, Tea, Floral Motif

(472) 5¼" Handled Vase, Cream Luster

(473) 5¾" Handled Urn Vase, Mottled Green Luster

(474) 7½" Double Vase Iridescent Yellow with Iridescent White Bird

(475) 5½" Urn Vase, Tan Luster

(476) 5½" Handled Vase Yellow Luster with Black Handles

(477) 4½" Cat Handle Creamer, Yellow Iridescent

(478) 4¼" Cat Handle Creamer, White Iridescent

(479) 4¼" Cat Handle Creamer, White Iridescent

(480) 5¾" Figurine, Bird, White Iridescent

(481) 4" Creamer, Lavender and White Luster

(482) 4¼" Teapot, Mottled Green Luster

(483) 4½" Creamer, Cream Luster

(484) 4¼" Covered Sugar, White Iridescent with Black Trim

(485) 4½" Canister, White Iridescent, Cloves

(486) 4½" Canister, White Iridescent, Cinamon (Spelling used by Czechs on this particular piece)

(487) 5¼" Figurine, Bird, White Luster with Scarlet Trim

(488) 5¼" Figurine, Bird, White Iridescent with Scarlet Trim

489

490

491

490

492

493

494

495

496

497

498

499

500

501

(489) 6¼" Vase, White, Erphila

(490) 6¼" Pair Candle Holders, White and Floral

(491) 10½" Handled Vase, Pink and White, Erphila

(492) 6¼" Vase, White

(493) 5" Pair of Book Ends, Pink and White

(494) 6" Figurine, Girl with Basket, Blue and White

(495) 2½" Powder Box, Blue and White, Eichwald

(496) Snack Set, Plate 8" Cup 2", Pink

(497) 4½" Handled Vase, Birds on White with
Black Trim

(498) 3" Box, Red, White and Blue with Butterfly
Finial

(499) 3½" Cup, Lavender, Blue and Gold

(500) 3½" Cup, Lavender, Blue and Gold

(501) 5" Basket, Floral

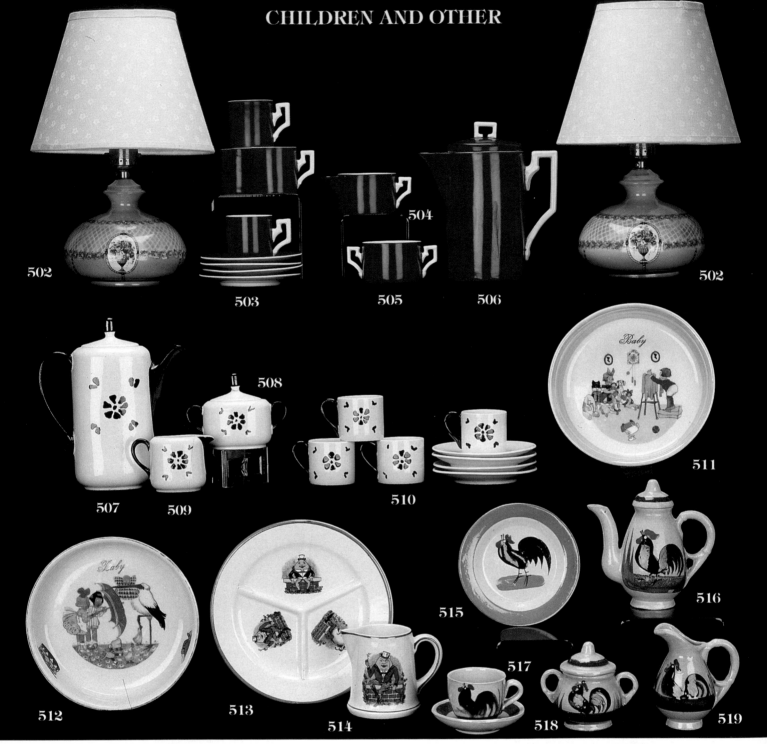

502

503

504

505

506

507

508

509

510

511

512

513

514

515

516

517

518

519

(502) 5¼" Pair of Lamps, Rose Floral, Tan and Green, New Shades

(503) 2" Cups and Saucers, Scarlet and White, Child's Set

(504) 2" Creamer, Scarlet and White, Child's Set

(505) 2" Open Sugar, Scarlet and White, Child's Set

(506) 6¾" Chocolate Pot, Scarlet and White, Child's Set

(507) 7¼" Chocolate Pot, White and Black, Child's Set

(508) 3¼" Covered Sugar, White and Black, Child's Set

(509) 2½" Creamer, White and Black, Child's Set

(510) 2" Cups and Saucers, White and Black, Child's Set

(511) 1¾" Baby Bowl, Gold and Tan Luster, Children and Toys

(512) 1¾" Baby Bowl, Orange and White, Stork, Baby and Children

(513) 7¼" Divided Baby Plate, Humpty Dumpty

(514) 3½" Creamer, Humpty Dumpty

(515) 4¼" Plate, Rooster, Brown and Green to Child's Set

(516) 5¼" Teapot, Rooster, Brown and Green to Child's Set

(517) 2" Cup and Saucer, Rooster, Brown and Green to Child's Set

(518) 3¼" Covered Sugar, Rooster, Brown and Green to Child's Set

(519) 4" Creamer, Rooster, Brown and Green to Child's Set

All pieces white background with exotic bird motif
Sets came in service for 4, 6, 8 or 12 and Open Stock

(520) 16" Platter
(521) 10" Platter
(522) 14" Platter
(523) 6½" Plate, Bread and Butter
(524) 8" Breakfast Plate
(525) 10" Dinner Plate
(526) 1½" Vegetable

(527) 4" Covered Vegetable
(528) 4" Covered Vegetable
(529) 3" Covered Butter
(530) 3" Creamer
(531) 1½" Soup
(532) 3" Sauce Boat
(533) 4" Covered Sugar
(534) 2" Cup and Saucer
(535) 6½" Plate, Bread and Butter

All pieces cream color background, with iris, rose and daisy motif.

Sets came in service for 4, 6, 8 or 12 and Open Stock

(536) 16" Platter
(537) 14" Platter
(538) 8" Square Breakfast Plate
(539) 10" Dinner Plate
(540) 5¼" Covered Vegetable

(541) 1½" Soup
(542) 1¼" Fruit Dish
(543) 3" Sauce Boat
(544) 1½" Vegetable
(545) 2¼" Vegetable
(546) 4" Covered Sugar
(547) 3" Creamer
(548) 2" Cup and Saucer
(549) 6½" Plate, Bread and Butter

All pieces white and cream background with basket of flowers Border Gold Trim

Sets came in service for 4, 6, 8 or 12 and Open Stock

(550) 14½" Platter
(551) 8" Square Breakfast Plate
(552) 6¼" Plate, Bread and Butter
(553) 9" Dinner Plate

(554) 2" Vegetable
(555) 2¼" Cup and Saucer
(556) 2" Handled Soup with Underplate
(557) 5½" Covered Vegetable
(558) 1½" Fruit Dish
(559) 3" Creamer
(560) 4" Covered Sugar

Pieces from two sets above (561) through (567),
   Large Rose Motif
(568) through (577), Flower and Violet Motif,
   Edna is name of pattern
These sets came in service for 4, 6, 8 or 12 and
   Open Stock

(561) 9" Dinner Plate
(562) 6¼" Bread and Butter
(563) 8" Breakfast Plate
(564) 12" Platter
(565) 2" Cup and Saucer

(566) 4¼" Covered Sugar
(567) 4" Creamer
(568) 3½" Sauce Boat
(569) 6½" Bread and Butter
(570) 4" Covered Sugar
(571) 3¼" Creamer
(572) 2½" Vegetable
(573) 4¼" Covered Vegetable
(574) 2" Cup and Saucer
(575) 13¾" Platter
(576) 9" Dinner Plate
(577) 8" Breakfast Plate

These pieces represent four different patterns of China
Sets came in service for 4, 6, 8 or 12 and Open Stock
(578) through (584) and (587) through (590) Small
    floral motif with gold trim, named Stephanie
(585) through (586) Dainty pink roses motif with gold
    trim, named Bordeaux
(591) Exotic Bird Motif, Named Eden
(592) through (599) Semi-Porcelain, Named Chelsea.
    Impressive Overall Pattern in Yellow

(578) 13½" Platter
(579) 2¼" Cup and Saucer
(580) 10" Dinner Plate
(581) 7½" Breakfast Plate
(582) 6½" Bread and Butter
(583) 3" Covered Sugar

(584) 3" Creamer
(585) 10" Dinner Plate
(586) 2¼" Cup and Saucer
(587) 2½" Vegetable
(588) 3½" Sauce Boat
(589) 1½" Soup
(590) 1¼" Fruit Dish
(591) 9½" Octagon Shape Plate
(592) 2" Vegetable
(593) 3" Egg Cup
(594) 1" Fruit Dish
(595) 2½" Handled Soup with Underplate
(596) 10" Dinner Plate
(597) 8½" Breakfast Plate
(598) 6½" Bread and Butter
(599) 2" Cup and Saucer

600   601   602   603   604

605   606   607   608

609   610   611   612   613   614

Complete 15 Piece Kitchen Set in Colorful Scarlet, Yellow, Blue and Lavender with Black on Off White Background.

(600) 8¾" Vinegar
(601) 7½" Rice
(602) 7½" Barley
(603) 7½" Oatmeal
(604) 8¾" Oil
(605) 6½" Salt

(606) 7½" Sugar
(607) 7½" Tea
(608) 7½" Coffee
(609) 4" Allspice
(610) 4" Cinnamon
(611) 4" Cloves
(612) 4" Ginger
(613) 4" Nutmeg
(614) 4" Pepper

70

Complete 15 Piece Kitchen Set, Border Design with Single Pink Rose, Off White Background and Gold Trim.

(615) 8½" Vinegar
(616) 6½" Coffee
(617) 6½" Sugar (Lid Missing)
(618) 6½" Prunes
(619) 8½" Oil
(620) 6" Salt

(621) 6½" Tea
(622) 6½" Oatmeal
(623) 6½" Rice
(624) 4" Allspice
(625) 4" Nutmeg
(626) 4" Ginger
(627) 4" Cloves
(628) 4" Mace
(629) 4" Cinnamon

630   631   632   633   634

635   636   637   638

639   640   641   642   643   644

Complete 15 Piece Kitchen Set, Orange, Yellow, Blue and Lavender with Black on Off White Background

(630) 8¾" Vinegar
(631) 7½" Oatmeal
(632) 7½" Flour
(633) 7½" Rice
(634) 8¾" Oil
(635) 6½" Salt

(636) 7½" Sugar
(637) 7½" Tea
(638) 7½" Coffee
(639) 4" Cloves
(640) 4" Cinnamon
(641) 4" Pepper
(642) 4" Nutmeg
(643) 4" Allspice
(644) 4" Ginger

Novelties and Seafood Dinner Sets of Four

(645) 7" Batter Spoon Holder, Blue, Pink and
Cream Figural Lady
(646) 5¼" Bank, Figural Pear, Erphila
(647) 3¼" Sauce with Under Plate Green
(648) 6" Juice Extractor, Lemon Figural, Yellow
(649) 6" Juice Extractor, Orange Figural, Orange
(650) 3½" Large Crab Covered Dish, Scarlet

(651) 2¼" Fish Covered Dish, Scarlet
(652) 3¼" Lobster Sauce
(653) 3" Lobster Covered Dishes, Scarlet, Three
Pictured
(654) 2" Crab Covered Dishes, Scarlet, Set of Four
(655) 1¾" Crab Salt and Pepper, Scarlet
(656) 9½" Dinner Plate with Lobster and Crab
Motif, Scarlet on Cream
(657) 2¾" Lobster Salt and Pepper, Scarlet

(658) 8¼" Plate, Strawberries, Cream and Scarlet
(659) 8¼" Plate, Apple, Cream and Yellow
(660) 8¼" Plate, Plums, Cream and Blue
(661) 8¼" Plate, Cherries, Cream and Scarlet
(662) 8¼" Plate, Orange, Cream and Orange
(663) 8¼" Plate, Grapes, Cream and Purple
(664) 6" Teapot, Exotic Bird, White and Orange
(665) 4¼" Covered Sugar, Exotic Bird, White and Orange

(666) 2½" Creamer, Exotic Bird, White and Orange
(667) 2" Cup and Saucer, Exotic Bird, White and Orange
(668) 7" Plate, Exotic Bird, White and Orange
(669) 4½" Covered Sugar, Yellow, White and Floral
(670) 3¼" Creamer, Yellow, White and Floral
(671) 4½" Handled Vase, Scarlet with Blue
(672) 2¼" Bowl, Red, Blue, Green and Yellow, Basket of Flowers

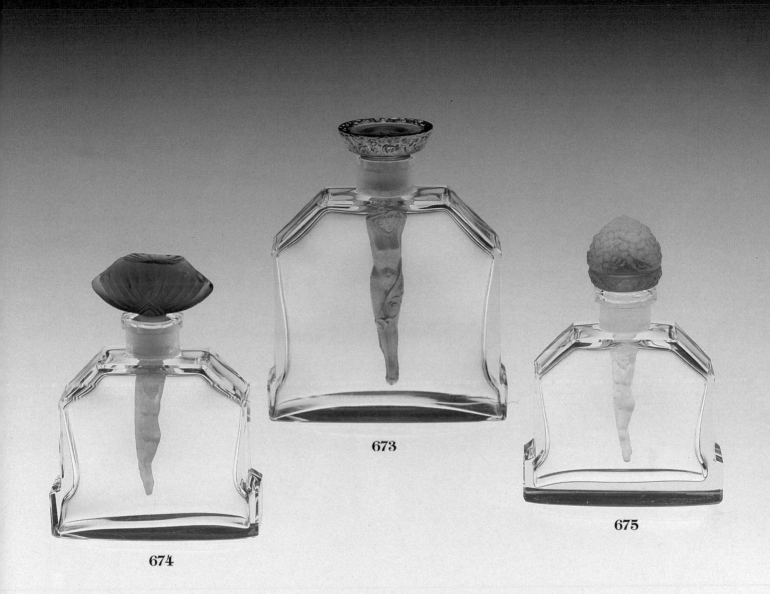

673

674

675

(673) 6¼" Clear, Turquoise Stopper with Turquoise Luster Nude Applicator

(674) 5¼" Clear, Blue Stopper with Blue Nude Applicator

(675) 5½" Clear, Pink Stopper with Clear Nude Applicator

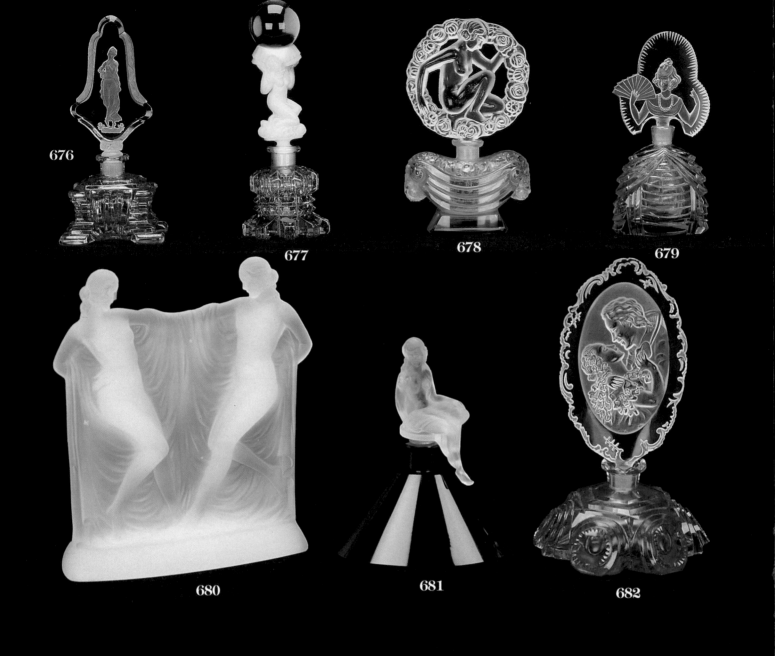

(676) 7" Blue, Clear and Frosted Lady Stopper

(677) 7½" Pink, Opaque White with Green Tint Nude Holding Glass Ball Stopper

(678) 6½" Pale Amber, Clear and Frosted Nude in Wreath Stopper

(679) 6¼" Green in Form of a Dress, Clear and Frosted Lady with Fan Stopper

(680) 8½" Opalescent Double Nude Statuette shown on the Vanity with the Perfume Bottles

(681) 6¾" Opaque Black, Frosted Sitting Nude Figural Stopper

(682) 8¾" Blue, Clear and Frosted Romantic Couple Stopper

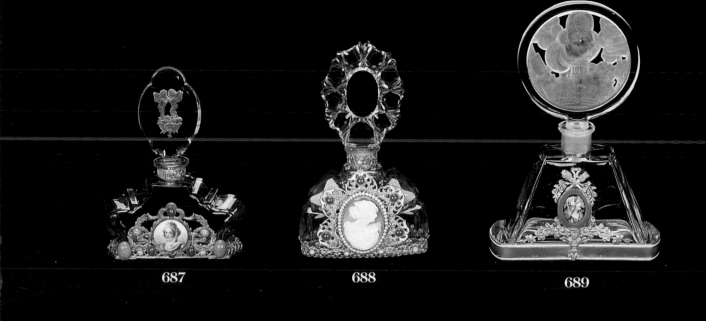

687   688   689

(683) 7¼" Blue, Clear and Frosted Girl by Tree
Stopper. Both Bottle and Stopper Em-
bellished with Brass and Jewel Ornamentation

(684) 4¼" Purple, Purple Stopper with Nude
Applicator

(685) 4½" Blue, Blue Venus de Milo Stopper

(686) 4¾" Clear and Frosted, Blue with Girl
Smoking Cigarette Stopper

(687) 5¾" Purple, Purple Stopper. Bottle has Brass
and Jewel Ornamentation with Portrait of
Queen Louise

(688) 6½" Blue, Blue Stopper. Bottle has Brass and
Jewel Ornamentation with Shell Cameo

(689) 7½" Clear, Clear and Frosted figure with two
Deer. Bottle has Brass and Jewel Ornamentation with Enameled Portrait. Ornamentation
is marked France.

(690) 8½" Opaque Aqua Floral, Opaque Aqua
      Stopper, Floral (Ingrid)
(691) 4¾" Opaque Black Floral, Tilted Bottle,
      Frosted Clear Stopper (Hoffman)
(692) 7" Pink, Pink Floral Stopper
(693) 3½" Opaque Black, Clear Stopper, Brass and
      Jewel Ornamentation
(694) 7¾" Opaque Black, Ivory Balcony Scene of
      Lovers with Dog Stopper
(695) 9" Opaque Aqua, Aqua Flower Basket
      Stopper (Ingrid)
(696) 5¾" Transparent Black Bottle and Stopper,
      Brass and Jewel Ornamentation
(697) 3½" Pink Bottle and Stopper
(698) 6½" Opaque Green Bottle and Stopper,
      Brass and Jewel Ornamentation

(699) 2½" Blue Bottle and Stopper
(700) 6¾" Opaque Black, Amber Stopper, Brass
      and Jewel Ornamentation (Hoffman)
(701) 3¾" Clear Bottle and Stopper, Brass and
      Jewel Ornamentation
(702) 6¼" Pink, Frosted and Clear Floral Stopper
(703) 2¾" Blue, Butterfly Shape, Clear Stopper,
      Brass and Jewel Ornamentation
(704) 5¾" Opaque Tan, Opaque Brown Stopper
(705) 5¼" Clear Ribbed, Blue Cut Fan Stopper
(706) 6¾" Clear Arched, Topaz Sunburst Stopper
(707) 5½" Aqua Opaque Nude, Floral Stopper (Ingrid)
(708) 7½" Crystal, Blue Floral Stopper
(709) 7¼" Crystal, Pink Ribbed and Floral Stopper

710   711   712   713   714   715

716   717   718   719

720   721   722   723   724

(710) 8¼" Frosted Black Bottle and Stopper (Ingrid)
(711) 9" Clear, Clear Prism Stopper, Brass and Jewel Ornamentation
(712) 7" Turquoise, Girl in Stopper, Brass and Jewel Ornamentation
(713) 5¾" Red, Clear and Frosted Tiara Stopper
(714) 8½" Purple, Clear and Frosted Floral Stopper
(715) 10" Blue Cut Bottle and Stopper
(716) 5½" Topaz, Floral Frosted Tiara Stopper
(717) 5½" Topaz, Figure in Stopper

(718) 6½" Topaz, Figure of Bo-Peep in Stopper
(719) 6" Amber Frosted Birds, Amber Clear Birds Stopper (Ingrid)
(720) 8" Pink, Clear and Frosted Girl Stopper
(721) 6¾" Clear, Clear and Frosted Bird Stopper
(722) 12" Clear and Frosted Three Dancing Nudes, Red Prism Stopper
(723) 6" Pink, Clear Stopper, Brass and Jewel Ornamentation
(724) 7¾" Clear, Butterfly and Flowers Stopper

725   726   727   728

729   730   731   732   733

(725) 7" Transparent Brown, Nude in Sea Shell
Stopper (Ingrid)

(726) 6" Clear, Clear Stopper, Brass and Jewel
Ornamentation

(727) 6" Clear, Double Nude Figures, Brass and
Jewel Ornamentation

(728) 7¼" Cobalt Blue, Figure in Stopper

(729) 10½" Clear, Clear Floral Stopper

(730) 8" Clear, Nude with Cornucopia Stopper
(Horn from Goat Amalthaea)

(731) 11½" Clear, Couple Sitting on Bench in the
Garden Stopper

(732) 7½" Clear, Scantily Draped Nude with Fish
Stopper

(733) 8" Clear, Girl Picking Flowers Stopper

(734) 7½" Red Atomizer, Mottled Colors
(735) 7¼" Blue Atomizer, Gold and Enamel Trim with Jewel Top
(736) 3½" Lavender Atomizer
(737) 6" Frosted Clear Atomizer with Painted Decoration and Opaque Green Foot
(738) 7¼" Red Atomizer, Mottled Colors
(739) 6" Pale Blue Atomizer, Enameled Pink Rose and Yellow Base
(740) 8¾" Red Atomizer
(741) 8¼" Pale Green and Clear Atomizer, Enameled Flowers with Green Jewel Top

(742) 6" Pale Yellow Atomizer, Blue Band with White Enamel Decoration
(743) 11¼" Frame with Mirror
6" Atomizer, Orange, Brass Trim
3⅛" Powder Box, Orange, Brass Trim
6¼" Bottle, Orange, Brass Trim
Complete Set
(744) 7½" Mercury Atomizer
(745) 8½" Opaque Green Atomizer, Red Bands, White Enamel, Crystal Jewel Top

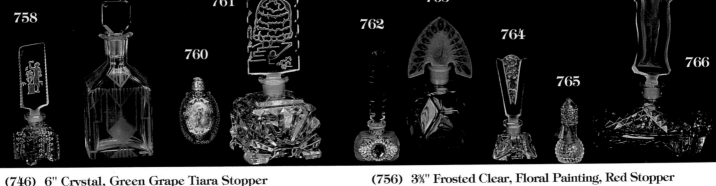

(746) 6" Crystal, Green Grape Tiara Stopper

(747) 6¾" Purple, Brass and Jewel Ornamentation, Purple with Frosted Cherubs Standing on a Rose, Stopper

(748) 10¾" Green Bottle and Stopper

(749) 5¼" Blue, Blue with Frosted Girl and Flowers Stopper

(750) 7¾" Pink, Frosted Pink Stopper with Head of Medea the Enchantress (Hoffman)

(751) 7¾" Clear, Transparent Black Lady Figure Stopper

(752) 6¼" Pink, Bottle and Stopper, Brass and Jewel Ornamentation on Bottle

(753) 8¼" Topaz Bottle and Stopper, Brass and Jewel Ornamentation on Bottle and Stopper (Amalthaea)

(754) 7¼" Transparent Black Bottle and Stopper, Brass and Jewel Ornamentation on Bottle

(755) 1¾" Transparent Black, Brass and Jewel Ornamentation

(756) 3¾" Frosted Clear, Floral Painting, Red Stopper

(757) 4½" Transparent Black

(758) 4¼" Blue, Brass and Jewel Ornamentation, Clear Stopper with Figure

(759) 5½" Vaseline, Clear Stopper

(760) 2½" Clear, Brass, Jewel and Portrait Ornamentation

(761) 7½" Clear Bottle and Stopper, Girl at Door with Bouquet on Stopper

(762) 4" Frosted Topaz, Clear Topaz Stopper, Brass and Jewel Ornamentation

(763) 4¾" Purple, Purple Peacock Stopper, Frosted and Clear

(764) 3½" Topaz, Clear and Frosted Stopper

(765) 2¼" Clear, Brass and Jewel Ornamentation Stopper (Stubby)

(766) 7½" Pink, Clear Frosted Nude Stopper

(767) 5½" Blue, Blue Stopper Cut Design on Bottom

(768) 6¼" Pink, Clear and Frosted

(769) 9" Blue, Blue Stopper

(770) 7" Pink, Clear Frosted Stopper

(771) 5¾" Blue, Blue Stopper

(772) 4¼" Green, Green Stopper, Brass and Jewel Ornamentation on Bottle

(773) 5" Green, Green Stopper, Brass and Jewel Ornamentation on Bottle

(774) 3½" Clear, Purple Base and Stoppers, Twin Set

(775) 4" Opaque Black, Pink Opaque Stopper with Bird (Hoffman)

(776) 4¼" Opaque Black, Clear Stopper, Brass and Jewel Ornamentation

(777) 2½" Green and Gold (Moser)

(778) 2½" Pink, Pink Stopper, Brass and Jewel Ornamentation

(779) 2" Topaz, Brass and Jewel Ornamentation

(780) 2½" Cranberry, Brass with Blue Top (Moser)

(781) 2¼" Clear, Brass with Dangling Beads (Stubby)

(782) 3" Clear, Red Glass Stopper

(783) 6¼" Opaque Black, Clear and Frosted Stopper, Brass and Jewel Ornamentation

(784) 4½" Clear, Clear Stopper, Brass and Jewel Ornamentation

(785) 6" Clear, Clear and Frosted Floral Stopper

(786) 6¼" Clear, Clear and Frosted Stopper of Woman and Man

(787) 6½" Pale Green, Clear and Frosted Stopper with Birds

(788) 7½" Clear Bottle and Stopper

(789) 6¾" Clear Bottle and Stopper

(790) 7¼" Blue, Clear and Frosted Stopper of Tropical Birds, Brass and Jewel Ornamentation on Bottle

(791) 6" Blue, Blue Floral and Butterfly Stopper (Ingrid)

(792) 6" Green Bottle and Stopper for Paris Decorators

(793) 6½" Opaque Red Floral Bottle and Stopper (Ingrid)

(794) 7½" Blue Bottle and Stopper

(795) 9" Opaque Green, Flower Basket Stopper, Brass and Jewel Ornamentation

(796) 7¼" Purple, Frosted Stopper, Figure and Two Deer

(797) 5½" Blue, Blue Stopper of Phrixus Riding Ram - Golden Fleece

(798) 5½" Green, Frosted Clear Stopper, Brass and Jewel Ornamentation on Bottle

(799) 5¼" Purple, Clear Stopper, Brass and Jewel Ornamentation on Bottle

(800) 5½" Turquoise Bottle and Stopper (Hoffman)

(801) 7¼" Purple Bottle and Stopper

(802) 2¼" Opaque Green

(803) 2½" Clear with Red Stopper

(804) 2½" Opaque Blue

(805) 3" Hawthorne, Glass Top Over Stopper

(806) 1¾" Opaque Black, Brass and Jewel Ornamentation

(807) 3" Purple Frosted, Brass Cap with Jewel on Top

(808) 2" Clear, Brass and Jewel Ornamentation

(809) 2¾" Enamel, Brass and Jewels

(810) 4½" Pink, Nude in Stopper (Hoffman)

(811) 5¾" Clear, Blue Cupid Stopper

(812) 8½" Topaz, Clear Butterfly and Flower Stopper, Bottle has Brass and Jewel Ornamentation

(813) 3½" Clear Bottle and Stopper

(814) 2" Clear with Jewel Top

(815) 3½" Amethyst Bottle and Stopper with Dancing Girl Throwing Flowers

(816) 6½" Clear, Frosted Green Stopper with Nude Sitting in Leaves (Ingrid)

(817) 5½" Red Frosted, Clear and Frosted Stopper
(818) 6¼" Opaque Black, Frosted Clear Stopper (Hoffman)
(819) Clear, Clear and Frosted Palm Tree Stopper, Bottle Brass and Jewel Ornamentation
(820) 9" Opaque Black, Opaque Red Nude Woman Stopper
(821) 4¼" Red Bottle and Stopper
(822) 7½" Opaque Black, Frosted and Clear Zephyr Lily Stopper
(823) 5¼" Red, Crystal Stopper
(824) 5½" Pink, Pink Figure Stopper
(825) 2¼" Opaque Blue
(826) 5¾" Green, Frosted Clear Stopper
(827) 3" Pink Bottle and Stopper

(828) 4" Blue Bottle and Stopper
(829) 6¼" Pink Bottle and Stopper
(830) 6" Blue, Clear and Frosted Stopper
(831) 3¼" Pink Bottle and Stopper with Figures (Hoffman)
(832) 4¼" Green Bottle and Stopper with Cupid
(833) 5" Clear Bottle and Stopper Portrait of Lady in Stopper
(834) 4¾" Clear, Clear and Frosted Lacy Stopper
(835) 7" Blue, Frosted and Clear Snowflake Stopper
(836) 5½" Opalescent Bottle and Stopper, Nude Figure on Bottle (Ingrid)
(837) 7½" Clear Cut Bottle, Blue Stopper
(838) 3" Clear Frosted Birds and Flowers, Kissing Birds Stopper
(839) 5" Clear Cut Bottle and Tiara Stopper

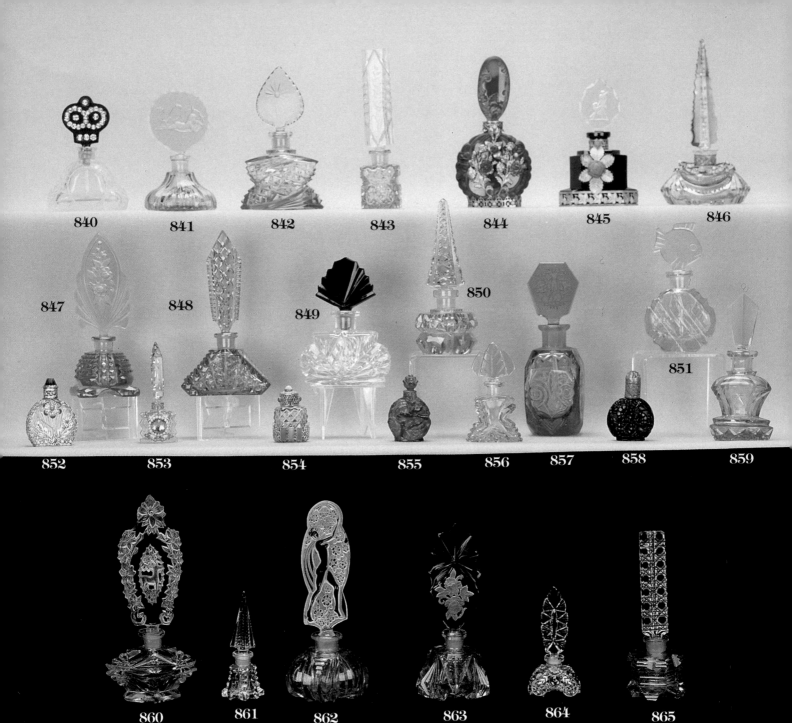

(840) 4½" Clear, Opaque Black Rhinestone Stopper
(841) 4¾" Blue, Frosted and Clear Stopper with Nude Figure - Boy
(842) 5¾" Green, Bottle and Stopper
(843) 6" Blue, Bottle and Stopper
(844) 6" Green Opaque Bottle and Stopper, Brass and Jewel Ornamentation on Bottle
(845) 5¼" Opaque Black, Clear and Frosted Stopper, Brass and Jewel Ornamentation on Bottle
(846) 6½" Topaz, Bottle and Stopper, Brass and Jewel Ornamentation on Bottle
(847) 6¼" Blue, Bottle and Stopper
(848) 6" Amber, Bottle and Stopper
(849) 4½" Clear, Opaque Black Stopper
(850) 5¾" Blue, Bottle and Stopper
(851) 4¾" Pink, Pink Fish Stopper
(852) 2¾" Clear, Brass and Jewel Ornamentation on Bottle and Stopper

(853) 3½" Blue, Bottle and Stopper, Brass and Jewel Ornamentation on Bottle
(854) 2" Amethyst, Brass and Jewel Ornamentation Over All
(855) 2½" Opaque Blue, Lapis
(856) 3½" Blue, Bottle and Stopper
(857) 6½" Purple, Bottle and Stopper with Figures
(858) 2½" Opaque Black, Brass and Green Stopper
(859) 5" Green, Bottle and Stopper
(860) 7" Pink, Bottle and Stopper with Deer
(861) 3½" Clear, Green Stopper
(862) 6½" Blue, Frosted and Clear Stopper with Nude Figure
(863) 6" Pink, Pink Stopper with Frosted Roses
(864) 3¾" Clear, Bottle and Stopper, Brass and Jewel Ornamentation on Bottle
(865) 5½" Purple, Clear Stopper

(866) 6¼" Blue, Clear with Frosted Birds Stopper
(867) 5¼" Blue, Bottle and Stopper
(868) 6" Blue, Bottle and Stopper
(869) 6½" Blue, Clear and Frosted Stopper
(870) 8½" Blue, Clear and Frosted Stopper, Brass and
Jewel Ornamentation
(871) 5¾" Blue, Bottle and Stopper (Ingrid)
(872) 5½" Blue, Bottle and Stopper
(873) 3¼" Opaque Black, Clear and Frosted Stopper,
Brass and Jewel Ornamentation
(874) 4½" Clear, Red Stopper
(875) 4½" Opaque Black, Clear and Frosted Stopper,
Brass and Jewel Ornamentation

(876) 4¾" Clear, Red Stopper
(877) 6½" Opaque Black, Clear Stopper, Brass and
Jewel Ornamentation
(878) 4½" Clear, Red Stopper
(879) 3¼" Opaque Black, Clear and Frosted Stopper
(880) 4" Clear, Blue Stopper
(881) 5¼" Amber, Bottle and Stopper with Figures
(882) 6¼" Clear and Frosted, Bottle and Stopper
(883) 6¼" Amber, Bottle and Stopper
(884) 8" Clear, Clear and Frosted Stopper
(885) 5½" Topaz, Crescent Topaz Stopper, Brass and
Jewel Ornamentation
(886) 3¼" Clear and Frosted, Gray Frosted Stopper

(887) 5¾" Topaz, Bottle and Stopper, Cherubs on Rose Stopper, Brass and Jewel Ornamentation on Bottle

(888) 6" Opaque Red, Crystal Stopper

(889) 4" Ivory, Bottle and Stopper

(890) 4½" Blue, Bottle and Stopper, Jewel and Brass Ornamentation on Bottle

(891) 5½" Amber, Bottle and Stopper

(892) 6¼" Pink, Bottle and Stopper

(893) 5¼" Transparent Black, Czech. Commercial, Desiree La Valliere

(894) 5½" Pink, Bottle and Stopper

(895) 4¼" Transparent Black, Peacock Stopper

(896) 7" Pink, Bottle and Stopper

(897) 3" Opaque Black Brass and Jewel Ornamentation Bottle and Top

(898) 4" Pink, Bottle and Stopper, Brass and Jewel Ornamentation

(899) 4" Purple, Clear and Frosted Stopper

(900) 6¼" Topaz, Bottle and Stopper, Brass and Jewel Ornamentation

(901) 7¾" Clear, Frosted Stopper, Raised Gold Decoration on Bottle and Stopper

(902) 6" Purple, Bottle and Stopper, Frosted Boy Playing Horn in Bottle

(903) 6¼" Topaz, Bottle and Stopper, Brass and Jewel Ornamentation on Bottle

(904) 3½" Blue, Clear and Frosted Stopper

(905) 2½" Clear, Brass and Jewel Ornamentation Over Bottle and Top

(906) 9¼" Black, Tinted Silver Leaping Nude with Stylized Butterfly Wings and Antenna
(907) 8" Pink, Pink Floral Stopper
(908) 7¾" Blue, Bottle and Stopper
(909) 6¾" Green, Bottle and Stopper
(910) 9¾" Red, Clear Stopper with Woman and Child
(911) 5" Green, Green Frosted Stopper, Brass and Jewel Ornamentation on Bottle
(912) 3¼" Pink, Pink Stopper with Rose, Brass and Jewel Ornamentation on Bottle
(913) 4¾" Blue Butterfly Shape Bottle, Blue Stopper with Frosted Clover
(914) 2¾" Clear, Red Stopper
(915) 5¾" Tan Opaque, Molded Opaque Brown Stopper (Hoffman)

(916) 3" Amber, Amber Jewel Top
(917) 6½" Blue 3-sided, Blue Dimensional Stopper
(918) 3¾" Pink, Bottle and Stopper
(919) 5½" Green, Clear and Frosted Nude Stopper, Brass and Jewel Ornamentation on Bottle
(920) 5" Clear Ship, Pink Sails
(921) 9" Clear and Frosted, Clear Open Stopper, Three Herons on Front of Bottle
(922) 3" Clear with Purple Stopper
(923) 6" Clear, Clear and Frosted Stopper
(924) 4" Clear with Red Stopper
(925) 6¼" Clear, Clear and Frosted Stopper of Woman Holding Cornucopia and Standing on a Butterfly
(926) 6" Clear, Clear and Frosted Stopper with Rose

927   928   929   930   931   932

933   934   935   936   937   938   939

940   941   942   943   944   945

(927) 7" Pink Bottle and Stopper
(928) 7¼" Purple Bottle and Stopper, Stopper
       Venus de Milo (Hoffman)
(929) 8¾" Pink Bottle, Clear Stopper
(930) 7½" Blue Bottle, Clear and Frosted Stopper
       of Girl with Flower
(931) 7" Blue, Clear and Frosted Stopper
(932) 7¼" Pink Clear Stopper
(933) 5½" Blue, Clear and Frosted Stopper
(934) 3¾" Pink Bottle and Stopper
(935) 3¾" Blue, Clear Stopper

(936) 4¾" Pink Bottle and Stopper
(937) 3½" Blue Bottle and Stopper
(938) 4¼" Blue with Clear Stopper
(939) 5¼" Blue Bottle and Feather Stopper
(940) 5" Blue with Clear Stopper
(941) 5¾" Clear with Red Stopper
(942) 2¼" Clear with Brass and Jewel
       Ornamentation
(943) 4½" Clear and Frosted, Red Stopper
(944) 5½" Clear with Red Stopper
(945) 5" Blue with Clear and Frosted Stopper

(946) 6½" Opaque Blue Bottle and Stopper

(947) 6¼" Aventurine Atomizer

(948) 7" Blue Atomizer

(949) 6¼" Blue with Gold Decoration Atomizer

(950) 5¾" Aqua Bottle and Stopper

(951) 5¼" Blue Bottle and Stopper

(952) 5" Purple with Clear Stopper

(953) 4½" Purple Frosted Bottle and Stopper

(954) 5¼" Purple Bottle and Stopper

(955) 6½" Purple Frosted Bottle and Stopper

(956) 6¾" Blue Bottle and Stopper

(957) 5¾" Blue Bottle and Stopper, Frosted Flower in Bottle

(958) 2¼" Topaz Bottle and Stopper

(959) 4¾" Blue with Clear Stopper

(960) 4¾" Blue with Blue Stopper

(961) 4¾" Blue with Clear Stopper, Brass and Jewel Ornamentation on Bottle

(962) 2" Topaz with Clear Stopper

(963) 5¾" Blue with Clear and Frosted Stopper

(964) 6¼" Clear with Blue Stopper

(965) 6¼" Clear Bottle and Stopper

(966) 7¾" Clear Bottle and Stopper

(967) 7¾" Clear Bottle and Stopper

(968) 7½" Clear Bottle and Stopper

(969) 6¾" Clear Bottle with Topaz Frosted Floral Stopper

(970) 5½" Clear with Pink Stopper

(971) 4½" Clear with Blue Stopper

(972) 6" Clear Bottle and Stopper

(973) 6½" Clear Bottle and Stopper

(974) 5" Clear Bottle and Stopper, Frosted Figures in Stopper, Minuet Couple

(975) 5½" Clear with Topaz, Frosted Figures in Stopper, Minuet Couple

(976) 5½" Clear with Pink Stopper

(977) 4¾" Clear Atomizer

(978) 5" Clear with Brass and Jewel Intaglio Cut Stopper

(979) 5" Clear Atomizer with Brass and Jewel Ornamentation Stopper

(980) 3¼" Clear with Topaz Stopper

(981) 2¼" Clear with Brass and Jewel Top and Dangling Beads (Stubby)

(982) 5" Clear Atomizer

(983) 2½" Powder Box, Pink with Clear Frosted Embossed Floral Lid, with Puff

(984) 16" Long Mirror, Brass, Frosted Embossed Floral Top

(985) 7¼" Pink with Frosted Clear Embossed Floral Pierced Stopper- Matches 983 and 984

(986) 5" Pink Bottle and Stopper

(987) 2¾" Green Bottle and Stopper

(988) 5¾" Green Bottle with Clear Stopper

(989) 4½" Pink Bottle and Stopper

(990) 5¾" Green Bottle with Clear Stopper

(991) 5¾" Pink Bottle and Stopper

(992) 4¼" Amber Bottle and Stopper

(993) 2½" Clear with Amber Stopper

(994) 5" Black Opaque Bottle with Clear Frosted Venus de Milo Stopper (Hoffman)

(995) 2½" Black Opaque with Clear Stopper

(996) 4½" Black Opaque with Clear and Frosted Stopper with Figure

(997) 2" Blue with Brass and Jewel Ornamentation on Bottle and Stopper

(998) 4" Blue with Clear and Frosted Floral Stopper, Brass and Jewel Ornamentation on Bottle

IDENTICAL BOTTLES IN DIFFERENT COLORS AND STYLES

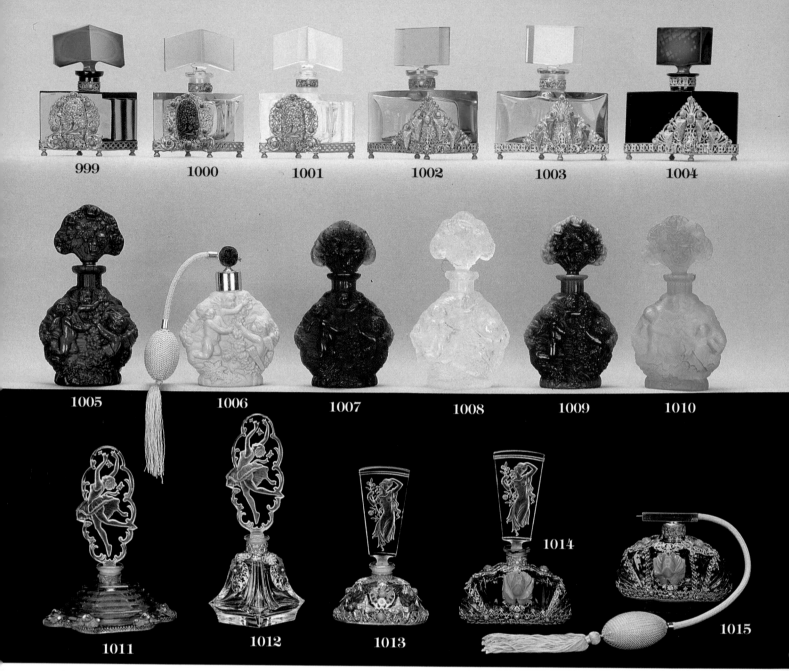

999 1000 1001 1002 1003 1004

1005 1006 1007 1008 1009 1010

1011 1012 1013 1014 1015

Top Row: Identical except for color or style
Middle Row: The same bottle in five different colors #1010 was made in Japan. Note lack of detail in raised figures. Fortunately, Made in Japan bottles are usually marked.
Bottom Row: Two each of the same stoppers with different bases.

(999)   5¾" Black Opaque with Green Opaque Stopper, Brass and Jewel Ornamentation
(1000)   5¾" Blue with Blue Stopper, Brass and Jewel Ornamentation
(1001)   5¾" Clear with Clear Stopper, Brass and Jewel Ornamentation
(1002)   5¾" Green Bottle and Stopper, Brass and Jewel Ornamentation
(1003)   5¾" Pink Bottle and Stopper, Brass and Jewel Ornamentation
(1004)   5¾" Black Opaque with Green Opaque Stopper, Brass and Jewel Ornamentation
(1005)   6½" Deep Blue Opaque Bottle and Stopper with Raised Figures

(1006)   5½" Opaque Aqua Atomizer with Raised Figures
(1007)   6½" Amberina Bottle and Stopper with Raised Figures
(1008)   6½" Clear Frosted Bottle and Stopper with Raised Figures
(1009)   6½" Amberina Opaque Bottle and Stopper with Raised Figures
(1010)   6½" Blue Frosted Bottle and Stopper with Raised Figures (Japan)
(1011)   6½" Pink, Clear Stopper with Frosted Figure, Brass and Jewel Ornamentation on Bottle
(1012)   7½" Clear, Clear Stopper with Frosted Figure, Brass and Jewel Ornamentation on Bottle
(1013)   5¾" Clear, Clear Stopper with Frosted Figure, Brass and Jewel Ornamentation on Bottle
(1014)   6¼" Green, Clear Stopper with Frosted Figure, Brass and Jewel Ornamentation on Bottle
(1015)   3½" Pink Atomizer, Brass and Jewel Ornamentation on Bottle

94

BIBLIOGRAPHY

Forsythe, Ruth A., *Made in Czechoslovakia*; Richardson Printing Corp., Marietta, Ohio, 1982

Glass Review, *Czechoslovak Glass and Ceramics Magazine*, 11/1899 Vol 1XXXXIII

Mrazek, Bill and Congressman Robert Mrazek, *A Piece of Mrazek History in Exhibition*;
   Northport Historical Society and Northport Museum, *The Long Islander*, February 6, 1992

North, Jacquelyne Y. Jones, *Czechoslovakian Perfume Bottles and Boudoir Accessories*; Antique
   Publications, Marietta, Ohio, 1990

North Jacquelyne Y. Jones, *Perfume Cologne and Scent Bottles*; Schiffer Publishing Ltd., West
   Chester, Pennsylvania, 1986

Northport Historical Society Museum, Northport, NY 1992

Pottery Glass & Brass Salesman, January 2, 1930

Prchal, Charles M., Highlights of Czech History American Sokol Educational and Physical
   Culture Organization, 1979

Smith, Burt, *Unraveling the Mysteries of Czechoslovakian Porcelain*, Mass Bay Antiques 1991

Wadsworth, Beula Mary, *Peasant Art in Czechoslovakia*; The School Arts Magazine, April, 1929

IS IT CZECHOSLOVAKIAN?

All items in this book are marked Czechoslovakia unless noted otherwise. In your search for these treasures, you will find many pieces that are not marked.

To add to the confusion, glass factories and pottery factories all over the world have copied Czechoslovakian design and color, and they have done an excellent job in some cases. For the most part, the copy is easy to detect because of poor quality.

Except for the Indians, every person in the United States is an immigrant or descended from immigrants. After World War I, European workers continued to crowd aboard ships bound for the United States. Many of these workers were Czechoslovakian and they looked for work that they had been trained to do in the homeland. They brought ideas and skills with them that were often helpful in whatever line of work they were experienced. Many went to work on farms, some worked in the steel mills, while others acquired work in the glass and pottery factories.

The above situations took place in other countries, hence we have the Czechoslovakian look in products that were made in Germany, France, Japan, Italy and other countries.

The true Czechoslovakian collector wants objects that were made in Czechoslovakia. If items are marked, anyone can determine if they are Czechoslovakian.

Differentiating reproductions from originals is a matter of experience. Only an expert can tell the difference, but you too can become an expert in time.